Reading Peak 2

NE_Build & Grow

Unit Components

Student Book

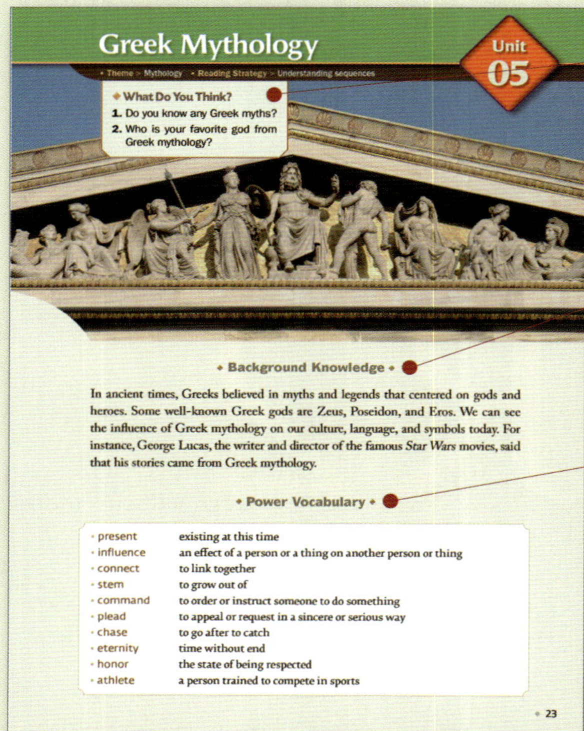
Greek Mythology

Unit 05

• Theme > Mythology • Reading Strategy > Understanding sequences

◆ What Do You Think?

1. Do you know any Greek myths?
2. Who is your favorite god from Greek mythology?

◆ Background Knowledge ◆

In ancient times, Greeks believed in myths and legends that centered on gods and heroes. Some well-known Greek gods are Zeus, Poseidon, and Eros. We can see the influence of Greek mythology on our culture, language, and symbols today. For instance, George Lucas, the writer and director of the famous *Star Wars* movies, said that his stories came from Greek mythology.

◆ Power Vocabulary ◆

present	existing at this time
influence	an effect of a person or a thing on another person or thing
connect	to link together
stem	to grow out of
command	to order or instruct someone to do something
plead	to appeal or request in a sincere or serious way
chase	to go after to catch
eternity	time without end
honor	the state of being respected
athlete	a person trained to compete in sports

23

What Do You Think?

Simple warm up questions and related images stimulate students' interest in each topic.

Background Knowledge

Background information is presented to better prepare students for the main readings.

Power Vocabulary

Key words from the main reading passage are carefully chosen and defined to build up students' understanding of the context.

Reading Comprehension

Multiple-choice and short-answer questions are introduced to ensure the students' understanding of the passages.

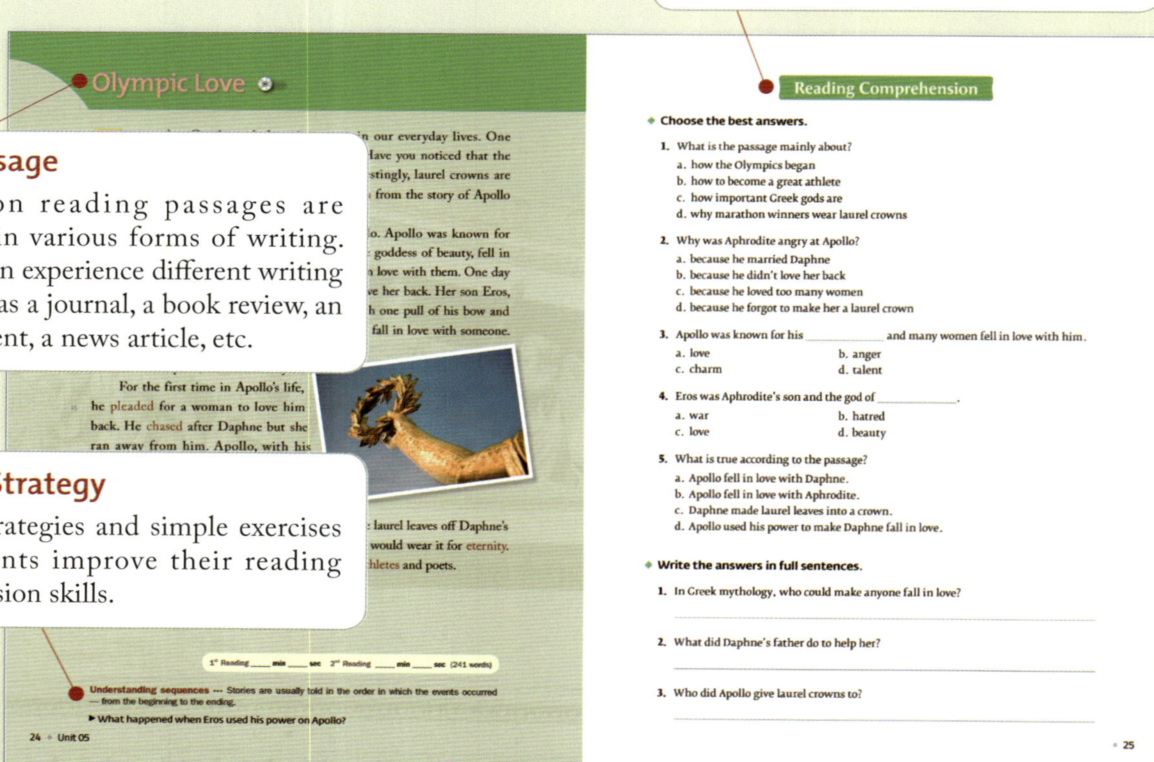
Olympic Love

... in our everyday lives. One ... have you noticed that the ... stingly, laurel crowns are ... from the story of Apollo

... o. Apollo was known for ... goddess of beauty, fell in ... love with them. One day ... e her back. Her son Eros, ... h one pull of his bow and ... fall in love with someone.

For the first time in Apollo's life, he pleaded for a woman to love him back. He chased after Daphne but she ran away from him. Apollo, with his ...

... laurel leaves off Daphne's ... would wear it for eternity. ... hletes and poets.

1st Reading ___ min ___ sec 2nd Reading ___ min ___ sec (241 words)

Understanding sequences --- Stories are usually told in the order in which the events occurred — from the beginning to the ending.

▶ What happened when Eros used his power on Apollo?

24 • Unit 05

Reading Comprehension

◆ Choose the best answers.

1. What is the passage mainly about?
   a. how the Olympics began
   b. how to become a great athlete
   c. how important Greek gods are
   d. why marathon winners wear laurel crowns
2. Why was Aphrodite angry at Apollo?
   a. because he married Daphne
   b. because he didn't love her back
   c. because he loved too many women
   d. because he forgot to make her a laurel crown
3. Apollo was known for his ________ and many women fell in love with him.
   a. love b. anger
   c. charm d. talent
4. Eros was Aphrodite's son and the god of ________.
   a. war b. hatred
   c. love d. beauty
5. What is true according to the passage?
   a. Apollo fell in love with Daphne.
   b. Apollo fell in love with Aphrodite.
   c. Daphne made laurel leaves into a crown.
   d. Apollo used his power to make Daphne fall in love.

◆ Write the answers in full sentences.

1. In Greek mythology, who could make anyone fall in love?
2. What did Daphne's father do to help her?
3. Who did Apollo give laurel crowns to?

25

Main Passage

Nonfiction reading passages are presented in various forms of writing. Students can experience different writing styles such as a journal, a book review, an advertisement, a news article, etc.

Reading Strategy

Reading strategies and simple exercises help students improve their reading comprehension skills.

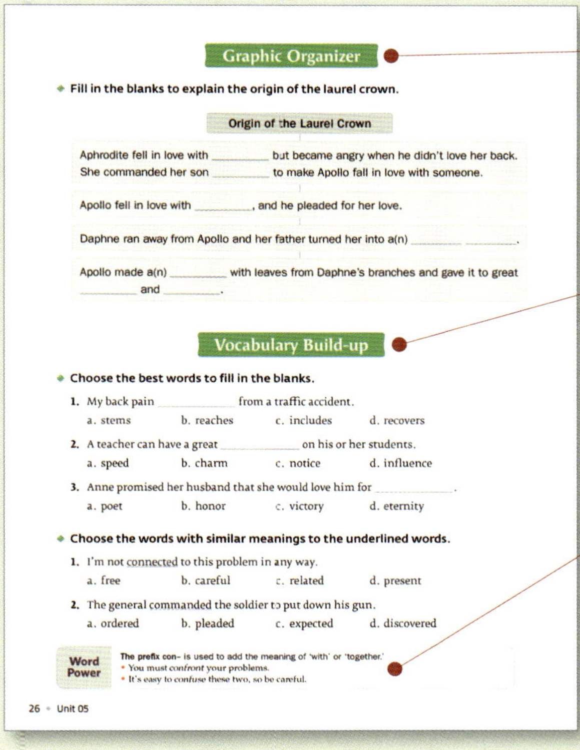

Graphic Organizer

◆ Fill in the blanks to explain the origin of the laurel crown.

Origin of the Laurel Crown

Aphrodite fell in love with ________ but became angry when he didn't love her back. She commanded her son ________ to make Apollo fall in love with someone.

Apollo fell in love with ________, and he pleaded for her love.

Daphne ran away from Apollo and her father turned her into a(n) ________ ________.

Apollo made a(n) ________ with leaves from Daphne's branches and gave it to great ________ and ________.

Vocabulary Build-up

◆ Choose the best words to fill in the blanks.

1. My back pain ________ from a traffic accident.
   a. stems b. reaches c. includes d. recovers
2. A teacher can have a great ________ on his or her students.
   a. speed b. charm c. notice d. influence
3. Anne promised her husband that she would love him for ________.
   a. poet b. honor c. victory d. eternity

◆ Choose the words with similar meanings to the underlined words.

1. I'm not connected to this problem in any way.
   a. free b. careful c. related d. present
2. The general commanded the soldier to put down his gun.
   a. ordered b. pleaded c. expected d. discovered

Word Power The prefix con- is used to add the meaning of 'with' or 'together.'
- You must confront your problems.
- It's easy to confuse these two, so be careful.

26 ◦ Unit 05

Graphic Organizer

Graphic organizers help students summarize the information from the main reading passages logically.

Vocabulary Build-up

Additional multiple-choice questions further strengthen students' vocabulary acquisition.

Word Power

The uses of different prefixes, suffixes, and root words are explained with more examples.

Writing Practice

Grammar and writing practice enhance students' writing skills.

Workbook

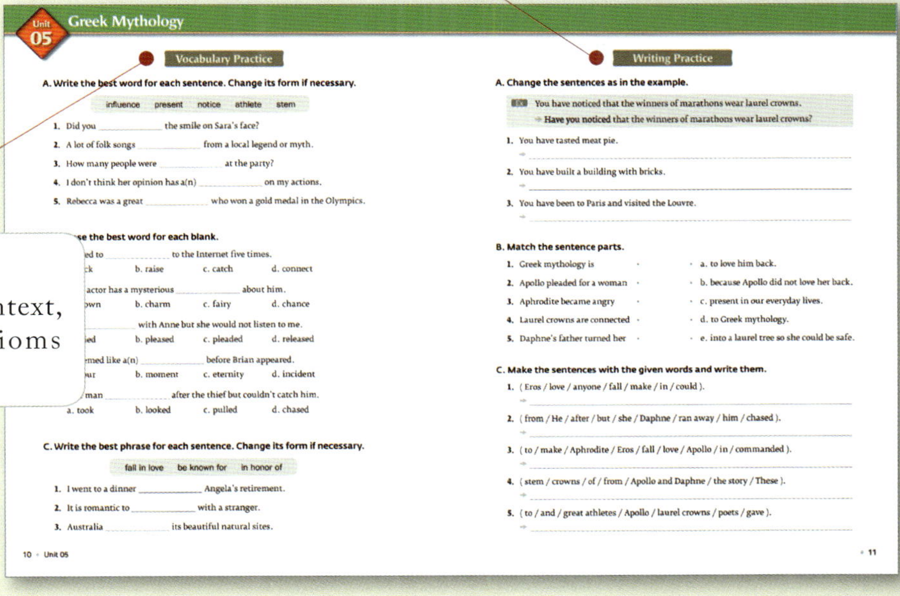

Unit 05 Greek Mythology

Vocabulary Practice

A. Write the best word for each sentence. Change its form if necessary.

influence present notice athlete stem

1. Did you ________ the smile on Sara's face?
2. A lot of folk songs ________ from a local legend or myth.
3. How many people were ________ at the party?
4. I don't think her opinion has a(n) ________ on my actions.
5. Rebecca was a great ________ who won a gold medal in the Olympics.

B. Choose the best word for each blank.

Writing Practice

A. Change the sentences as in the example.

Ex. You have noticed that the winners of marathons wear laurel crowns.
→ Have you noticed that the winners of marathons wear laurel crowns?

1. You have tasted meat pie.
2. You have built a building with bricks.
3. You have been to Paris and visited the Louvre.

B. Match the sentence parts.

1. Greek mythology is · · a. to love him back.
2. Apollo pleaded for a woman · · b. because Apollo did not love her back.
3. Aphrodite became angry · · c. present in our everyday lives.
4. Laurel crowns are connected · · d. to Greek mythology.
5. Daphne's father turned her · · e. into a laurel tree so she could be safe.

C. Make the sentences with the given words and write them.

1. (Eros / love / anyone / fall / make / in / could).
2. (from / He / after / but / she / Daphne / ran away / him / chased).
3. (to / make / Aphrodite / Eros / fall / love / Apollo / in / commanded).
4. (stem / crowns / of / from / Apollo and Daphne / the story / These).
5. (to / and / great athletes / Apollo / laurel crowns / poets / gave).

C. Write the best phrase for each sentence. Change its form if necessary.

fall in love be known for in honor of

1. I went to a dinner ________ Angela's retirement.
2. It is romantic to ________ with a stranger.
3. Australia ________ its beautiful natural sites.

10 ◦ Unit 05 ◦ 11

Vocabulary Practice

Exercises on new words in context, synonyms, antonyms, and idioms improve students' vocabulary.

Scope and Sequence

Lie Detectors

Unit 01

• Theme > Psychology • Reading Strategy > Finding main ideas

◆ **What Do You Think?**

1. How can you tell if someone is lying?
2. Do you believe a machine can tell if people are lying?

◆ Background Knowledge ◆

When people lie, they usually want to keep it a secret. However, they often wish they knew when other people were lying. Throughout history, many cultures had tests to find out if someone was lying. For example, in West Africa, a group of people would pass around an egg. They thought that the person who broke the egg was guilty because he or she was nervous.

◆ Power Vocabulary ◆

- expression — the feelings shown on a person's face
- invent — to make something that has never been made before
- measure — to express as a number or quantity
- response — the reaction of a living thing to a stimulus
- innocent — having not done a bad act or crime
- guilty — the state of a person who has committed a crime
- permit — to allow something to happen
- evidence — something that can be used to prove something
- reject — to not accept
- department — a specialized part of a large organization

Truth or Lie? T01

Can you tell if someone is lying just by looking at their facial expressions? Think how useful it would be if you had a machine that could tell when a person was telling a lie! In the early 20th century, the polygraph, or lie detector was invented by John Larson and Leonarde Keeler.

The lie detecting process starts with an interviewer asking some basic questions. The polygraph measures the heartbeat, breathing, and sweating of the person being tested. Then the interviewer asks questions about a crime. When people are telling a lie, their body response will change because they feel nervous or worried. By comparing the different body response information, the polygraph can detect whether the person being tested is lying or not.

However, there is also a problem with using lie detectors. Sometimes, innocent people also get nervous when they have to take a lie detector test. The test may show that someone is guilty just because his or her body shows signs of stress. This is why most countries don't permit lie detector results as evidence in court.

Even though lie detectors are widely rejected by most countries, they are still used in some places. American police departments and government agencies, like the FBI or CIA, still use polygraphs to question suspects. Polygraphs help them in many ways, but no person or machine is able to detect lies 100 percent of the time.

1st Reading _____ min _____ sec 2nd Reading _____ min _____ sec (235 words)

Finding main ideas ··· The main idea of an article tells what it is mostly about.

▶ What is the main idea of this article?

Reading Comprehension

Choose the best answers.

1. What is the passage mainly about?

a. the study of crimes
b. the reason people lie
c. the usage of lie detectors
d. the way the body reacts to lying

2. When was the polygraph invented?

a. in the mid-19th century
b. in the late 19th century
c. in the mid-20th century
d. in the early 20th century

3. Lie detectors may show that a person is guilty just because of signs of ______________.

a. crime
b. stress
c. sorrow
d. questions

4. Which is NOT measured by a polygraph?

a. sweating
b. breathing
c. heartbeat
d. body movement

5. What can be concluded from the passage?

a. Polygraphs are not always accurate.
b. The police always know when people are lying.
c. Lie detectors aren't popular with the FBI or CIA.
d. Companies buy lie detectors to test their workers.

Write the answers in full sentences.

1. What happens when people are telling a lie?

____

2. Why do most countries NOT permit the results of polygraphs in court?

____

3. Where are lie detectors used these days?

____

Graphic Organizer

◆ **Fill in the blanks to explain how a polygraph works.**

How a Polygraph Works

1st step: An interviewer asks some __________ questions.

2nd step: The polygraph __________ the heartbeat, breathing, and sweating.

3rd step: The interviewer asks questions about a(n) __________.

4th step: The polygraph compares the different body __________ information.

Vocabulary Build-up

◆ **Choose the best words to fill in the blanks.**

1. I can ______________ the smell of smoke very well.

a. result b. detect c. explain d. response

2. It was proven that Eric was ______________ and he was released from prison.

a. nervous b. guilty c. innocent d. official

3. You shouldn't ______________ an idea just because it's different from your own.

a. lieb. tell c. reject d. breathe

◆ **Choose the words with similar meanings to the underlined words.**

1. Is there any <u>evidence</u> to support what you say?

a. signs b. proof c. motion d. problems

2. I can't forget Olivia's facial <u>expression</u> when I met her for the first time.

a. look b. stress c. machine d. research

Word Power

The suffix -ion is added to represent the "state" or "motion" of a verb.

- I don't know how to *express* my feelings.
- Rachel often uses artistic *expression*.

Ancient Greece

Unit 02

• Theme > History • Reading Strategy > Recalling facts and details

What Do You Think?

1. What was life like in ancient Greece?
2. What would life be like for a Spartan child?

Background Knowledge

In ancient Greece, different societies taught in different ways. Both Athenians and Spartans believed in the importance of education, but they concentrated on different subjects. Athenians focused on the arts. They taught poetry, music, and history, but only to boys. Spartans, on the other hand, focused on military matters and they taught both girls and boys.

Power Vocabulary

state	the condition of a person or thing
constant	continually happening, not changing
gain	to get something as a result of one's efforts
bear	to give birth to
courage	a power that enables someone to face danger without fear
loyalty	faithfulness to a king or queen, government, or belief
brutal	harsh or cruel
advantage	a better position or power
enemy	a person who hates or wishes to harm you
envy	to strongly want what someone else has

The Strength of Sparta

T02

Ancient Greece was continuously in a state of war. There were constant battles to gain land. To protect themselves, Spartans educated and trained their people for war.

The tough Spartan education was taught to both boys and girls and began the moment they were born. Soldiers checked newborn babies to see if they were physically fit enough to become a Spartan warrior. If they thought a baby was too weak, it was left to die.

At the age of seven, both boys and girls left their homes to go to school and get training. Girls went through physical training because Spartans believed that strong women would bear strong babies for their family and government. Also, when the men were out to war, girls and women had to protect their homes and land. Physically, it was harder for boys than girls at these schools. Spartans made boys eat too little food. Since food was sometimes difficult to find during wars, this let the boys get used to hunger. Also, boys joined the "Agoge," an educational system, which taught them war songs, hunting, history, and sports. This system encouraged the boys to build their courage and loyalty.

Though the training was brutal for children, Sparta produced the best warriors among the 20 polises[1] in ancient Greece. Their tough education was an advantage during times of war. Their enemies envied the power and strength of Sparta.

1 polis: a city-state in ancient Greece

1st Reading _____ min _____ sec 2nd Reading _____ min _____ sec (233 words)

Recalling facts and details ··· Facts and details explain more about the main idea with examples. They explain the who, what, where, when, why, and how of the main idea.

► How were Spartan boys taught?

Reading Comprehension

◆ **Choose the best answers.**

1. What is the passage mainly about?

a. the origin of war
b. Spartan education
c. the importance of education
d. the differences between Sparta and Athens

2. Ancient Greece was in a continuous state of ______________.

a. war
b. trade
c. peace
d. education

3. Which is NOT true according to the passage?

a. Spartan education was given only to boys.
b. Spartan women protected their homes during wars.
c. Spartans began their education when they were born.
d. Spartan education focused on physical strength and fighting skills.

4. When did Spartan children leave their homes to go to school?

a. at the age of five
b. at the age of three
c. at the age of seven
d. the moment they were born

5. Which was NOT taught in the "Agoge" educational system?

a. sports
b. geography
c. history
d. war songs

◆ **Write the answers in full sentences.**

1. What happened to Spartan babies who were NOT physically fit to become warriors?

____

2. Why did Spartan girls go through physical training?

____

3. Why did enemies envy the power and strength of Sparta?

____

Graphic Organizer

◆ **Fill in the blanks to compare Spartan education for boys and girls.**

Spartan Education

Boys	Girls
• Physically, boys had a(n) __________ time than girls. • Boys were made to eat too __________ food. • Boys joined the educational system "__________."	• Girls went through __________ training. • Women needed to be strong to bear __________ babies and to __________ their homes and land.

Vocabulary Build-up

◆ **Choose the best words to fill in the blanks.**

1. The government encourages women to ______________ many children.

a. leave b. bear c. join d. marry

2. By reading books, Andrew ______________ lots of knowledge.

a. showed b. checked c. trained d. gained

3. The army is fighting against their ______________ near the border.

a. friends b. battles c. enemies d. advantages

◆ **Choose the words with similar meanings to the underlined words.**

1. The crimes are getting more and more <u>brutal</u>.

a. cruel b. soft c. smooth d. smart

2. I don't have the <u>courage</u> to stand up to him.

a. mind b. bravery c. weakness d. strength

Word Power

The suffix -y is used with nouns or adjectives to show the state or result of an activity.

- Ted led our team to *victory*.
- Allie ate dinner, but now she's *hungry* again.

Beavers

Unit 03

• Theme > Animals • Reading Strategy > Recognizing cause and effect

What Do You Think?

1. What do beavers look like?
2. What is an important feature of beavers?

Background Knowledge

Beavers are the second largest rodents (a grouping of mammals which includes rats and mice) in the world. They are about 90 cm long and can weigh up to around 30 kg. Most people can recognize them by their large front teeth and thick brown fur. They also have a big scaly tail and webbed feet that help them survive in wetlands, like swamps.

Power Vocabulary

- glance — a quick look
- vital — absolutely necessary
- maintain — to keep in a certain state, position, or activity
- construct — to make by putting together materials and parts
- pile — to place things in layers
- gap — an open or empty space in or between things
- steady — not changing, especially in behavior
- flood — the overflowing of water
- entrance — the passage, door, or gate for entering
- endanger — to put someone or something in danger

Leave It to Beavers

T03

At first glance, the trees cut down by beavers seem to hurt the environment. But did you know that they actually play a vital role in the ecosystem? For thousands of years, beavers have maintained the health of water systems and animals by constructing dams and lodges.

Beavers use their powerful front teeth to cut down trees and other plants. Then they pile up the logs, branches, and leaves in a crisscross pattern to construct dams and lodges. Lastly, they carry mud in their front paws and teeth and use it to fill in the gaps.

Beavers build dams when the water levels are low in wetlands. These dams attract other animals that live in or near water. Beavers need dams to find food and protect them from enemies and natural disasters, such as floods. They maintain a steady water level and stop floods from destroying their homes.

When the water level is high enough, beavers build lodges. These homes have entrances underneath the water. Since it is difficult for other animals to swim underwater, the homes are safe places for beavers to live in.

The construction of dams and lodges provides safe homes for beavers and other animals to help them survive. Since almost half of all the endangered animals in the world live in wetlands, these animals simply need to leave it to beavers to build a good environment for them.

1st Reading _____ min _____ sec 2nd Reading _____ min _____ sec (233 words)

Recognizing cause and effect ··· The cause and effect are the reasons and the results of an event. The cause makes the effect happen.

▶ Why is it safe for beavers to live in lodges?

Reading Comprehension

Choose the best answers.

1. What is the passage mainly about?

a. the roles of dams
b. the development of water systems
c. the environmental problems of rivers
d. beavers' construction of dams and lodges

2. What does They refer to in the passage?

a. Beavers b. Dams
c. Water systems d. Animals

3. What is NOT true according to the passage?

a. Dams help other animals that live near water.
b. Dams create unsteady water levels and floods.
c. Beavers construct dams and lodges in a crisscross pattern.
d. Beavers can cut down trees and other plants with their front teeth.

4. Beavers build ______________ when the water level is high enough.

a. dams b. lodges
c. enemies d. natural disasters

5. Where are the entrances of lodges located?

a. on land
b. in dams
c. underground
d. underneath the water

Write the answers in full sentences.

1. What do beavers' dams attract?

____

2. Why do beavers need dams?

____

3. When do beavers build dams?

____

Graphic Organizer

◆ **Fill in the blanks to explain beavers' construction.**

Beavers' Construction

Dams	Lodges
• are built when the water levels are __________ • help beavers find __________ • protect beavers from __________ and natural __________	• are built when the water level is __________ enough • have __________ underneath the water • provide beavers __________ places to live in

Vocabulary Build-up

◆ **Choose the best words to fill in the blanks.**

1. We ______________ the books up on the shelves.

a. built b. piled c. threw d. destroyed

2. To ______________ good health, we must have a healthy diet.

a. attract b. protect c. maintain d. endanger

3. I couldn't find the ______________ to the theater in the dark.

a. role b. shape c. flood d. entrance

◆ **Choose the words with similar meanings to the underlined words.**

1. A mistake by a doctor can endanger a person's life.

a. build b. enter c. threaten d. construct

2. Robert played a vital role in the development of our community.

a. minor b. crucial c. pretty d. small

Word Power

The prefix en– is used to add the meaning of 'to make' or 'to put within.'
- You need to have the *courage* to state your opinion.
- The teacher tried to *encourage* the boy's musical talent.

Ultraviolet Light

Unit 04

• **Theme** > Science • **Reading Strategy** > Scanning

What Do You Think?

1. What color is light?

2. Why do we need sunscreen when we go out on sunny days?

Background Knowledge

A long time ago, people thought light was created by our eyes. But actually, it is made up of tiny particles of energy called photons. Some of these photons take the forms of waves. The length of the waves is also responsible for colors: different wavelengths make different colors.

Power Vocabulary

• ray	a column of light
• visible	capable of being seen
• cause	to make something happen
• cell	the basic structural unit of all organisms
• responsible	having control or authority over something
• surface	the top layer or outside part of something
• capable	able to do something; very good at doing a job
• severely	in a harsh or strict manner
• shield	a protective covering
• block	to stop from happening or developing

Stay Safe from Ultraviolet Light!

When you think about light, you might imagine a light bulb or the rays of the sun. These are examples of "visible light." There are actually many kinds of light, including ultraviolet, or UV, rays from the sun.

How is UV light different from normal light? It has shorter wavelengths than visible light and it has more energy, so it can pass through objects. It is harmful because it can cause changes in the cells of our bodies.

There are three kinds of UV rays: UVA, UVB, and UVC. But only UVA and UVB travel all the way to the Earth. UVB rays are responsible for most cases of sunburn, as they are shorter than UVA rays and only reach the surface of the skin. UVA rays are capable of passing into the skin deeper than UVB rays. They play a major role in the aging and wrinkling of the skin. Both UVA and UVB rays can cause skin cancer if they severely damage skin cells.

The ozone layer is like a gas shield around the Earth that blocks UV rays. But this doesn't mean we're perfectly safe from them. It's still important to wear sunscreen when you go outside. Sunscreen doesn't just protect you from sunburns. It can also protect your skin cells from the greater danger of skin cancer.

1st Reading _____ min _____ sec 2nd Reading _____ min _____ sec (222 words)

Scanning ··· When you search for specific information, you move your eyes quickly down the page seeking specific words and phrases.

▶ Which UV rays cause the aging and wrinkling of the skin?

Reading Comprehension

Choose the best answers.

1. What is the passage mainly about?

a. the effects of UV rays
b. the ways to cure cancer
c. the roles of the ozone layer
d. the invention of light bulbs

2. Which is NOT true according to the passage?

a. UV rays are responsible for sunburns.
b. UV rays are blocked by the ozone layer.
c. UV rays have more energy than visible light.
d. The wavelengths of UV rays are longer than visible light.

3. UV rays are harmful to humans because they ______________.

a. are not visible
b. can destroy the ozone layer
c. pollute the air with chemicals
d. can cause changes in the cells of our bodies

4. What rays are responsible for most cases of sunburn?

a. UVA
b. UVB
c. UVC
d. the sun's rays

5. What protects our skin from sunburns?

a. sunscreen
b. normal light
c. sunglasses
d. UVA and UVB rays

Write the answers in full sentences.

1. How is UV light different from normal light?

____

2. Which UV rays can pass deeper into the skin?

____

3. What are the two benefits of sunscreen?

____

Graphic Organizer

◆ **Fill in the blanks to compare visible light with UV light.**

Light	
Visible Light	**UV Light**
• has ________ wavelengths than UV light • has ________ energy than UV light	• causes changes in the ________ of our bodies • is responsible for ________ • ages and wrinkles the ________ • can cause skin ________

Vocabulary Build-up

◆ **Choose the best words to fill in the blanks.**

1. My brother ____________ many problems, but I love him.

a. causes b. damages c. passes d. imagines

2. All of us are ____________ for the problem and have to solve it.

a. safe b. normal c. capable d. responsible

3. Suddenly, one man ____________ my car on the street.

a. wore b. waved c. blocked d. traveled

◆ **Choose the words with similar meanings to the underlined words.**

1. I didn't notice any <u>visible</u> changes in the room.

a. huge b. critical c. detectable d. dangerous

2. The river has been <u>severely</u> polluted by factory waste.

a. little b. hardly c. slightly d. seriously

Word Power

The root word vis– has the meaning of 'to see.'
- I'm planning to *visit* my grandmother next week.
- The teacher used *visual* aids to highlight the key points of her lecture.

Greek Mythology

Unit 05

• **Theme** > Mythology • **Reading Strategy** > Understanding sequences

◆ **What Do You Think?**

1. Do you know any Greek myths?
2. Who is your favorite god from Greek mythology?

◆ Background Knowledge ◆

In ancient times, Greeks believed in myths and legends that centered on gods and heroes. Some well-known Greek gods are Zeus, Poseidon, and Eros. We can see the influence of Greek mythology on our culture, language, and symbols today. For instance, George Lucas, the writer and director of the famous *Star Wars* movies, said that his stories came from Greek mythology.

◆ Power Vocabulary ◆

- present — existing at this time
- influence — an effect of a person or a thing on another person or thing
- connect — to link together
- stem — to grow out of
- command — to order or instruct someone to do something
- plead — to appeal or request in a sincere or serious way
- chase — to go after to catch
- eternity — time without end
- honor — the state of being respected
- athlete — a person trained to compete in sports

Olympic Love

T05

Even today, Greek mythology is present in our everyday lives. One example of its influence is the Olympics. Have you noticed that the winners of marathons wear laurel crowns? Interestingly, laurel crowns are connected to Greek mythology. These crowns stem from the story of Apollo and Daphne.

This story begins with Aphrodite and Apollo. Apollo was known for his charm. Many women, including Aphrodite, the goddess of beauty, fell in love with him. He, on the other hand, did not fall in love with them. One day Aphrodite became angry because Apollo did not love her back. Her son Eros, the god of love, could make anyone fall in love with one pull of his bow and arrow. Aphrodite commanded Eros to make Apollo fall in love with someone. When Eros used his power, Apollo fell in love with Daphne, a beautiful fairy.

For the first time in Apollo's life, he pleaded for a woman to love him back. He chased after Daphne but she ran away from him. Apollo, with his athletic speed, caught up to her. She cried out to her father, the god of the river. He turned her into a laurel tree so she could be safe. Apollo was sad and heartbroken. He picked the laurel leaves off Daphne's branches, made them into a crown, and said that he would wear it for eternity. In honor of her, Apollo gave laurel crowns to great athletes and poets.

1st Reading ____ min ____ sec 2nd Reading ____ min ____ sec (241 words)

Understanding sequences ··· Stories are usually told in the order in which the events occurred — from the beginning to the ending.

▶ What happened when Eros used his power on Apollo?

Reading Comprehension

Choose the best answers.

1. What is the passage mainly about?

a. how the Olympics began
b. how to become a great athlete
c. how important Greek gods are
d. why marathon winners wear laurel crowns

2. Why was Aphrodite angry at Apollo?

a. because he married Daphne
b. because he didn't love her back
c. because he loved too many women
d. because he forgot to make her a laurel crown

3. Apollo was known for his ______________ and many women fell in love with him.

a. love　　b. anger
c. charm　　d. talent

4. Eros was Aphrodite's son and the god of ______________.

a. war　　b. hatred
c. love　　d. beauty

5. What is true according to the passage?

a. Apollo fell in love with Daphne.
b. Apollo fell in love with Aphrodite.
c. Daphne made laurel leaves into a crown.
d. Apollo used his power to make Daphne fall in love.

Write the answers in full sentences.

1. In Greek mythology, who could make anyone fall in love?

____

2. What did Daphne's father do to help her?

____

3. Who did Apollo give laurel crowns to?

____

Graphic Organizer

◆ **Fill in the blanks to explain the origin of the laurel crown.**

Origin of the Laurel Crown

- Aphrodite fell in love with __________ but became angry when he didn't love her back. She commanded her son __________ to make Apollo fall in love with someone.

- Apollo fell in love with __________, and he pleaded for her love.

- Daphne ran away from Apollo and her father turned her into a(n) __________ __________.

- Apollo made a(n) __________ with leaves from Daphne's branches and gave it to great __________ and __________.

Vocabulary Build-up

◆ **Choose the best words to fill in the blanks.**

1. My back pain ______________ from a traffic accident.

a. stems b. reaches c. includes d. recovers

2. A teacher can have a great ______________ on his or her students.

a. speed b. charm c. notice d. influence

3. Anne promised her husband that she would love him for ______________.

a. poet b. honor c. victory d. eternity

◆ **Choose the words with similar meanings to the underlined words.**

1. I'm not <u>connected</u> to this problem in any way.

a. free b. careful c. related d. present

2. The general <u>commanded</u> the soldier to put down his gun.

a. ordered b. pleaded c. expected d. discovered

Word Power

The prefix con– is used to add the meaning of 'with' or 'together.'

- You must *confront* your problems.
- It's easy to *confuse* these two, so be careful.

UFOs

Unit 06

• **Theme** > Mystery • **Reading Strategy** > Identifying an author's purpose

What Do You Think?

1. Do you think UFOs really exist?

2. What do UFOs look like?

Background Knowledge

The U.S. government first used the term UFO, which stands for "unidentified flying object," in a report in 1952. Even in 1896, however, people were talking about "mystery airships." The U.S. government tried to find out if these "flying saucers" were real, and if aliens were flying them. Although the government found no evidence of aliens, some people still believe in UFOs.

Power Vocabulary

- alien — a person or creature from a planet other than the Earth
- astronomer — someone who studies stars and planets using scientific equipment
- exist — to live; to have real being
- announce — to make known
- mistake — to have a wrong idea about someone or something
- debate — a formal discussion in which opposing arguments are put forward
- prove — to provide evidence for
- solid — thorough and reliable
- firm — not likely to change
- continue — to keep happening

Do UFOs Exist?

Magazine

Today, UFOs are usually just jokes we see in cartoons and movies. Most people don't believe that aliens have visited the Earth in spaceships. Scientists and astronomers lack evidence that UFOs don't exist, but they still say the existence of UFOs is extremely unlikely.

It wasn't long ago, though, that people were more serious about UFOs. The U.S. military received many reports of UFOs in the 1940s and 1950s. They tried to find out if aliens had really come to the Earth. In 1970, they announced that there was no evidence of UFOs. Still, some people think that the U.S. government did find proof of aliens, but that they hid the evidence.

Then again, most reports of UFOs are from people who don't know about astronomy. They could easily mistake a strange cloud, light, or airplane for an alien spaceship. Astronomers, on the other hand, are experts on the night sky. They look at it all the time, but no astronomer has ever reported seeing a UFO.

The problem with this debate is that it's almost impossible to prove that aliens have never visited the Earth. We do know that no one has ever found solid scientific evidence of an alien landing. Scientists and astronomers who study these kinds of things are very firm: UFOs are not alien spaceships. But that doesn't change things for the people who continue to believe.

1st Reading _____ min _____ sec 2nd Reading _____ min _____ sec (231 words)

Identifying an author's purpose ··· Authors share their attitudes on different subjects to explain, describe, entertain or persuade with their text.

▶ What does the author try to explain in the 3rd paragraph?

Reading Comprehension

Choose the best answers.

1. What is the passage mainly about?

a. the design of UFOs
b. aliens living on the Earth
c. proof that aliens exist
d. the debate over the existence of UFOs

2. ______________ think that the existence of UFOs is extremely unlikely.

a. Believers and nonbelievers
b. Government and politicians
c. Scientists and astronomers
d. Military generals and soldiers

3. Which is NOT true according to the passage?

a. No astronomer has ever reported seeing a UFO.
b. In 1970, the U.S. military announced that there was evidence of UFOs.
c. The U.S. military received many reports of UFOs in the 1940s and 1950s.
d. Most people don't believe that aliens have visited the Earth in spaceships.

4. According to the passage, who usually reports seeing UFOs?

a. People who have met aliens.
b. People who studied astrology.
c. People who are experts on the night sky.
d. People who don't know about astronomy.

5. According to the passage, what firm belief do scientists and astronomers have?

a. UFOs are studying humans.
b. UFOs are not alien spaceships.
c. UFOs have not visited the Earth.
d. UFOs visited the Earth a long time ago.

Write the answers in full sentences.

1. What do most people think about UFOs?

____

2. What do people mistake for an alien spaceship?

____

3. What is the problem with the UFO debate?

____

Graphic Organizer

◆ **Fill in the blanks to compare the two opinions about whether UFOs exist or not.**

Existence of UFOs

Believers	Experts
• think the U.S. government __________ the evidence of UFOs • easily mistake a strange cloud, light, or airplane for a(n) __________ __________	• have never __________ seeing a UFO • are __________ that UFOs are not alien spaceships

Vocabulary Build-up

◆ **Choose the best words to fill in the blanks.**

1. No life would ______________ without water.

a. die　　b. exist　　c. change　　d. separate

2. ______________ are trying to find out more about black holes.

a. Actors　　b. Detectives　　c. Physicians　　d. Astronomers

3. We are pleased to ______________ the birth of our son.

a. prove　　b. deny　　c. receive　　d. announce

◆ **Choose the words with similar meanings to the underlined words.**

1. The <u>debate</u> over the old issue has continued.

a. report　　b. evidence　　c. discussion　　d. astronomer

2. I hold the <u>firm</u> belief that I will succeed in this project.

a. soft　　b. light　　c. fixed　　d. extreme

Word Power

The root word astro– has a meaning related to 'stars' or 'space.'
- I want to be an *astronaut* and explore space.
- Ella thinks fortune telling and *astrology* are nonsense.

Five Senses

Unit 07

• Theme > Science • Reading Strategy > Using a graphic organizer

What Do You Think?

1. Which sense do you think is the most important?
2. Could you survive without your senses?

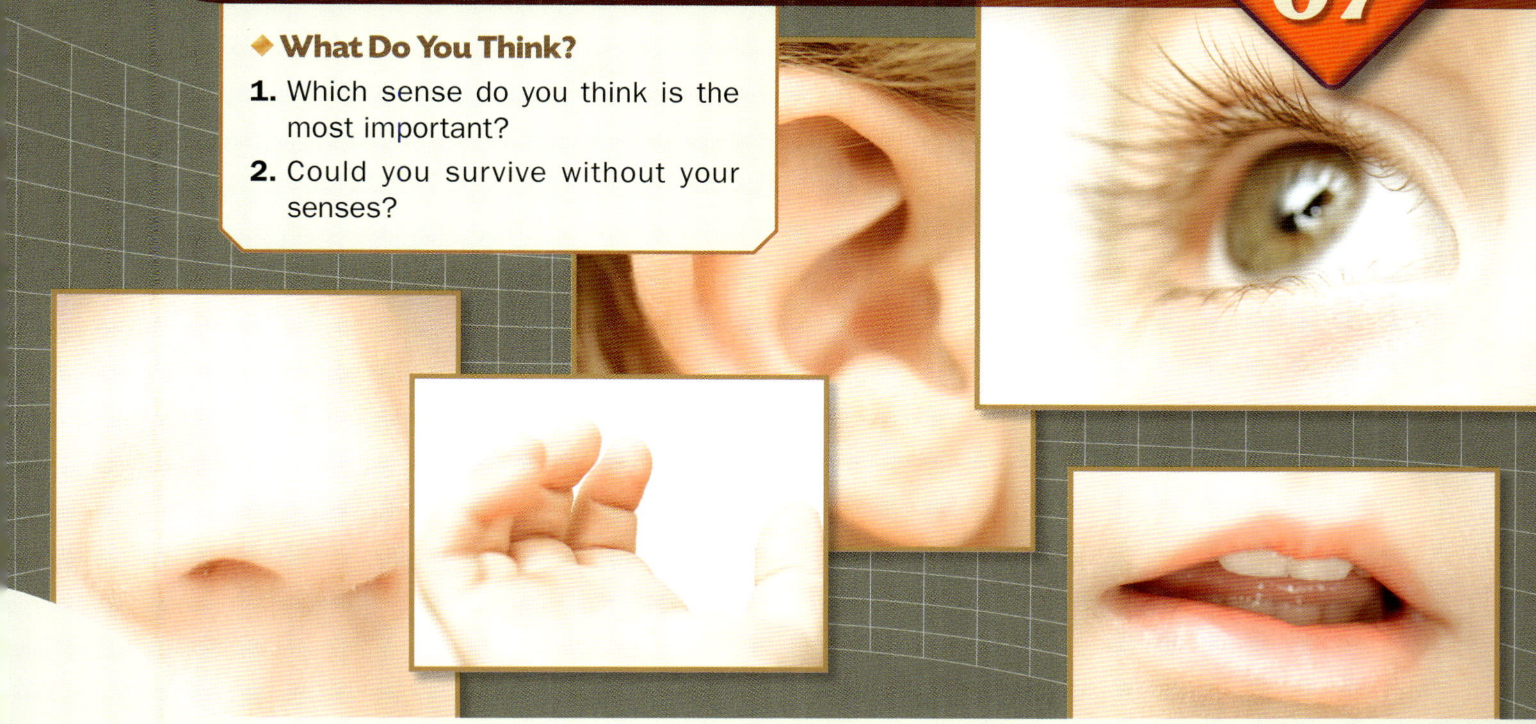

Background Knowledge

How do animals and humans experience the world outside of their own bodies? They use five senses: sight, hearing, smell, touch, and taste. The five senses are extremely important for their survival. Humans have come to use their senses less for survival with the invention of modern technology. However, like all creatures, we still need them to get around every day.

Power Vocabulary

• essential	completely necessary
• survive	to continue to live through hardship
• communication	the sharing or exchange of ideas, opinions, and information
• vary	to be different in some particular way
• depend	to have trust in
• superior	better than someone or something else in quality or skill
• creature	a living person or animal
• distinguish	to mark as different
• herd	a group of animals of the same type that live together
• recognize	to detect with the senses

Senses of Creatures

T07

Without senses, humans and animals would have a hard time trying to live in the world. Senses are essential in many ways. Senses help them survive through communication and escape from danger. Senses are also used to gather necessary things like food and water. We experience all five senses, but the role of each sense varies. Certain senses develop in a unique way depending on the type of environment a creature lives in.

We can take elephants' senses as an example. They have superior hearing, smell, and touch. Elephants talk to each other in a way that is beyond humans' hearing abilities. Their sounds help them escape from dangerous situations. In fact, their hearing is thought to be the best out of all the creatures on land.

Additionally, elephants' nostrils[1] are used to distinguish various herd members. Each animal has its own unique smell. When a mother elephant gives birth, she drops her baby elephant into a pile of her dung. She can then easily recognize her baby from this smell.

Elephants also have a superior sense of touch. They can feel vibrations in the ground. So, when thunder shakes the earth underneath them, they can tell where rainwater is.

Senses are essential for all creatures. The value of each sense, however, is different for every creature, according to its environment.

1 nostrils: the two outside openings of the nose

1st Reading _____ min _____ sec 2nd Reading _____ min _____ sec (221 words)

Using a graphic organizer ··· You can use different kinds of graphic organizers to arrange the information you have gained from a reading.

► Organize the senses of elephants.

Reading Comprehension

Choose the best answers.

1. What is the passage mainly about?

a. living without senses
b. the importance of senses
c. animals' communication
d. elephants' natural habitat

2. Which does NOT fit in the blank?

Elephants have a superior sense of ____________.

a. sight
b. touch
c. smell
d. hearing

3. How do elephants communicate with each other?

a. by feeling vibrations
b. by recognizing smells
c. by touching their nostrils
d. with sounds beyond humans' hearing

4. Which is NOT true according to the passage?

a. All elephants have the same smell.
b. Senses help creatures escape from danger.
c. The value of each sense varies depending on environment.
d. Elephants' nostrils are used to distinguish various herd members.

5. What can be concluded from the passage?

a. Animals can live without one sense.
b. Animals have superior senses to humans.
c. The senses of living things are important.
d. The senses of animals and humans are different.

Write the answers in full sentences.

1. What would life be like without our senses?

____

2. Why is elephants' hearing thought to be the best out of all the creatures on land?

____

3. How can a mother elephant recognize her baby?

____

Graphic Organizer

◆ **Fill in the blanks to explain elephants' senses.**

Elephants' Senses

Hearing	Smelling	Touch
• Elephants ___________ from dangerous situations using their superior hearing.	• Elephants use their nostrils to distinguish ___________ members.	• Elephants can feel ___________ in the ground and tell where ___________ is.

Vocabulary Build-up

◆ **Choose the best words to fill in the blanks.**

1. I saw a ___________ of cattle and I stopped my car.

a. herd   b. sense   c. smell   d. supply

2. Many people ___________ the importance of saving the environment.

a. listen   b. dislike   c. depend   d. recognize

3. We have to plan a diet that includes ___________ nutrients for our body.

a. creative   b. original   c. essential   d. dangerous

◆ **Choose the words with similar meanings to the underlined words.**

1. This product is popular because of its <u>superior</u> quality.

a. strange   b. special   c. unique   d. excellent

2. The twins were so much alike that I couldn't <u>distinguish</u> one from the other.

a. tell   b. escape   c. change   d. produce

Word Power

The prefix super– is used to add the meaning of 'over' or 'above.'

- Sally doesn't believe in *supernatural* powers.
- People can show *superhuman* power when faced with a crisis.

Operas Vs. Musicals

Unit 08

• **Theme** > Performing arts • **Reading Strategy** > Comparing and contrasting

◆ **What Do You Think?**

1. What kinds of performances have you experienced?
2. Have you heard of *The Phantom of the Opera*?

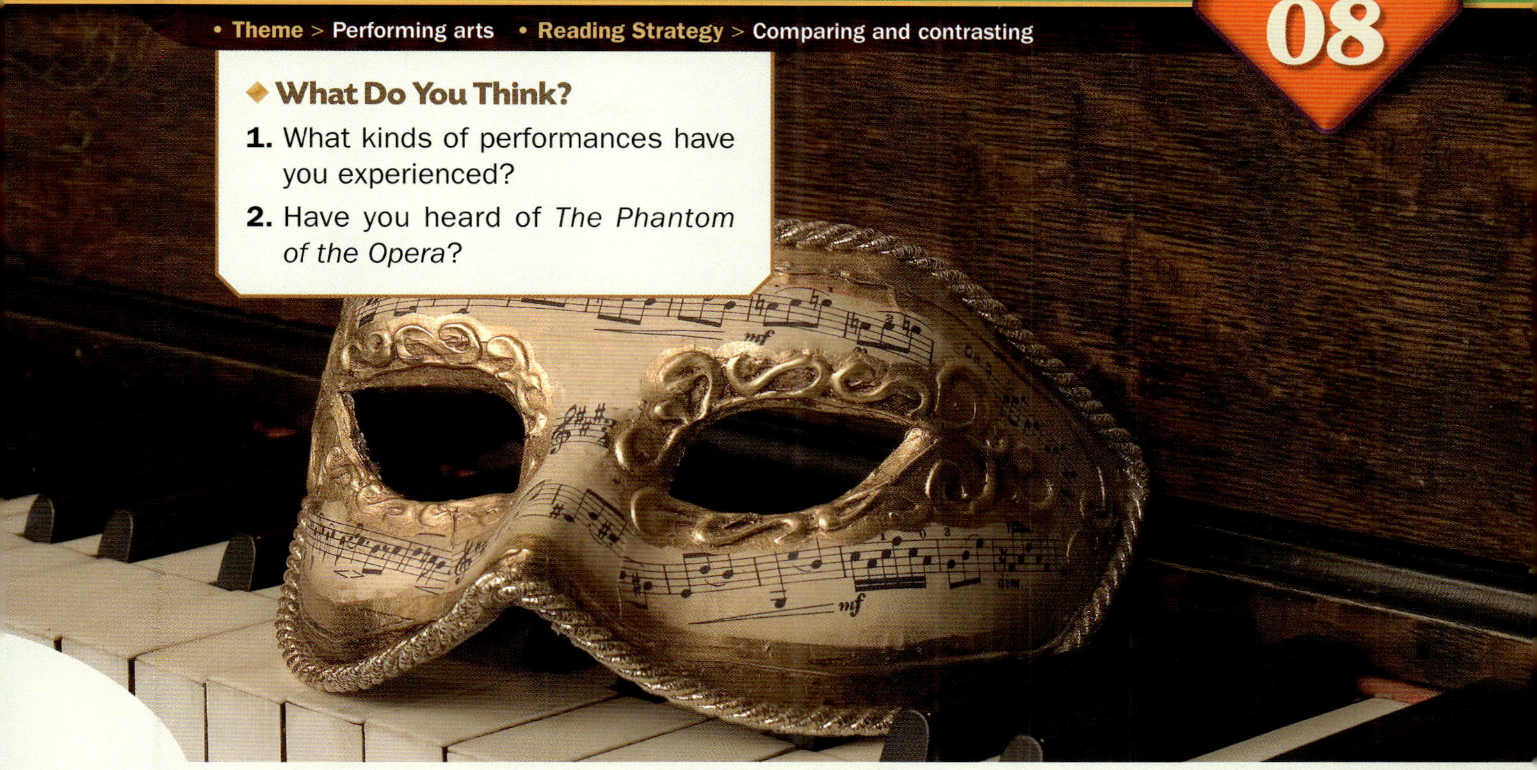

◆ Background Knowledge ◆

A theatrical performance is when people act out a story for an audience. It usually happens on a big stage and the performers typically wear costumes. They tell a story through actions, song, dance, or speech. There are two main types of theatrical performances. The first type are comedies or funny stories, and the second type are tragedies or sad stories.

◆ Power Vocabulary ◆

• perform	to act on a stage, on TV, or in a movie
• costume	a style of dress, including accessories and hairdos
• audience	a group of people who gather to watch or hear something
• composer	a person who writes music
• tragic	causing great sadness, because someone suffers or dies
• character	a person in a story, play, or film
• dialog	the lines spoken by characters in a drama or novel
• element	a part of something that makes up a whole
• inspire	to influence someone to do or create something
• fairly	to a degree that is not large but not small

Musical or Opera? T08

Have you ever heard of *The Phantom of the Opera*? Is it a musical or is it an opera? Both operas and musicals are performed with singing and costumes on a stage in front of an audience. But operas are much older than musicals. The first one was performed in 1598! Some modern composers still write operas, but most operas performed today were written before the 1920s. Operas aren't always serious, but the acting is usually very dramatic. The stories are usually very tragic, too. And the performers playing the characters sing the dialog very loudly because most opera houses don't have microphones.

Musicals, on the other hand, are a much newer form of entertainment. The first musicals were performed on Broadway in New York City, in 1879. They were called musical comedies. Most musicals are comical although they sometimes have some sad elements. Early musicals were inspired by operettas, or light operas, but they had more talking and dancing. Generally, musicals have a lighter vocal style than operas. And the music halls where they are performed today often have microphones.

Now think about *The Phantom of the Opera*. It has a lot of spoken dialog and the vocal style is fairly light. So, even though it is about a man living in an opera house, it is actually a musical.

1st Reading _____ min _____ sec 2nd Reading _____ min _____ sec (221 words)

Comparing and contrasting ··· Comparing and contrasting is used to show how certain things or ideas are similar or different from one another.

▶ How is the singing in operas different from the singing in musicals?

Reading Comprehension

Choose the best answers.

1. What is the passage mainly about?

a. the origin of opera
b. the singing style of musicals
c. the popularity of *The Phantom of the Opera*
d. the similarities and differences between operas and musicals

2. When was the first opera performed?

a. in 1598
b. in 1879
c. in the early 1920s
d. in the late 1920s

3. The acting in operas is usually very ______________.

a. comical
b. tragic
c. dramatic
d. modern

4. The first musicals were called ______________.

a. operettas
b. light operas
c. tragic dramas
d. musical comedies

5. Which is NOT true according to the passage?

a. In most operas, the dialog is sung very loudly.
b. *The Phantom of the Opera* is an opera.
c. Early musicals were inspired by operettas.
d. The first musicals were performed on Broadway.

Write the answers in full sentences.

1. Why must opera singers sing loudly?

____

2. When were the first musicals performed?

____

3. What is the vocal style of musicals like?

____

Graphic Organizer

◆ **Fill in the blanks to explain how operas and musicals are different.**

	Operas	Musicals
First Performance	• in ________	• in ________
Stories	• ________________	• ________________
Vocal Style	• ________ singing	• ________ singing

Vocabulary Build-up

◆ **Choose the best words to fill in the blanks.**

1. There was a large ____________ at the concert.

a. reason　　b. dialog　　c. theater　　d. audience

2. Mozart was one of the greatest ____________ in the world.

a. actors　　b. senses　　c. costumes　　d. composers

3. Health is an essential ____________ for happiness.

a. hall　　b. stage　　c. element　　d. ability

◆ **Choose the words with opposite meanings to the underlined words.**

1. Sarah had a <u>tragic</u> accident on the way home from work.

a. sad　　b. delightful　　c. sorrowful　　d. heartbreaking

2. My father <u>inspired</u> me to apply to the college.

a. stopped　　b. included　　c. surprised　　d. performed

Word Power

The suffix -er is used to show a person or a thing that does something.

- The deer was chased by the *hunter*.
- The *gardener* is planting some trees and flowers.

Ecotourism

Unit 09

• Theme > Travel • Reading Strategy > Distinguishing fact from opinion

◆ **What Do You Think?**

1. What was your favorite trip?
2. What do you usually do when you are traveling?

◆ Background Knowledge ◆

People usually travel for fun or to relax. They don't usually think of the environment while traveling. However, there is a special kind of tourism called ecotourism. The goal of ecotourism is to find environmentally friendly ways to explore and enjoy nature. It also helps local economies by bringing money to different areas.

◆ Power Vocabulary ◆

• reach	to arrive
• local	related to a particular area
• purchase	to buy something
• contribute	to give for a purpose
• landscape	an area of land that can be seen at one time from one place
• fuel	a substance that can be used to produce energy
• observe	to watch something with care in order to discover something
• pure	free from polluting matter
• preserve	to take care of something in order to prevent it from being harmed
• community	the people living in one area

Traveling to Heaven

T09

Travel Essay

Ecotourism is great for adventurers. It brings people to places that have not been changed by humans. I've always loved to travel and one of my dreams was to experience untouched nature. Not long ago, I was able to do that. My wife and I decided to go on an ecotourism trip to Charlevoix, Quebec. It was unforgettable!

When we reached our destination, our tour guide welcomed us. Before we began our adventure, he took us around the small shops and restaurants owned by local people. We purchased many beautiful handmade items at the local shops. We were delighted to contribute to the economy of the town since the profit went directly to the local people. The money we spent will help to preserve the beautiful landscape which was created almost 350 million years ago.

We then traveled into the area's untouched forests. To minimize the pollution, we traveled in a vehicle that ran on environmentally friendly fuel. We saw thick trees, clean riverbanks, and wild animals. It was exciting to observe nature in its pure state.

Looking back on our trip to Charlevoix makes me smile. I discovered the beauty of nature during the trip. I was also able to understand the importance of preserving our environment and local communities. One day, I hope ecotourism will help my children experience heaven on Earth like I have.

1st Reading _____ min _____ sec 2nd Reading _____ min _____ sec (227 words)

Distinguishing fact from opinion ··· A fact is something that is either true or untrue and can be proved. An opinion is a person's own view, judgment, or attitude. It is often expressed with 'I think,' 'I believe,' or 'in my opinion.'

► Find the facts about the writer's trip to Charlevoix.

Reading Comprehension

Choose the best answers.

1. What is the passage mainly about?

a. the role of tour guides
b. ways to support local communities
c. the economy of Charlevoix, Quebec
d. ecotourism as a valuable experience

2. What was one of the writer's dreams?

a. to buy handmade items
b. to own a small restaurant
c. to discover a beautiful place
d. to experience untouched nature

3. Which is NOT mentioned in the passage?

a. Tour guides make a lot of money from ecotourism.
b. The couple visited shops and restaurants owned by local people.
c. The landscape of Charlevoix, Quebec was created 350 million years ago.
d. The couple traveled in a vehicle that used environmentally friendly fuel.

4. How did the couple contribute to the economy of the area?

a. by taking pictures
b. by riding in an eco-friendly vehicle
c. by observing nature
d. by purchasing things at local shops

5. What did the couple NOT see in the untouched forests of Charlevoix?

a. wild animals
b. thick trees
c. camping sites
d. clean riverbanks

Write the answers in full sentences.

1. Why is ecotourism great for adventurers?

____

2. Where did the couple go during their trip?

____

3. How did the writer feel during the trip?

____

Graphic Organizer

◆ **Fill in the blanks to organize the passage about travel.**

Ecotourism in Charlevoix

Where the Writer Visited	• Charlevoix, Quebec
What the Writer Did	• visited the small shops and restaurants owned by ___________ people • traveled into untouched ___________ in a vehicle that ran on environmentally friendly fuel
How the Writer Felt	• was delighted to contribute to the ___________ of the town • was excited to observe nature in its ___________ state

Vocabulary Build-up

◆ **Choose the best words to fill in the blanks.**

1. ___________ food is usually fresh and healthy.

a. Local b. Human c. Beautiful d. Fermented

2. This car is not economical because it uses a lot of ___________.

a. trees b. fuel c. vehicles d. riverbanks

3. I can't forget the beautiful view of the ___________ from the mountain top.

a. items b. dreams c. landscape d. community

◆ **Choose the words with similar meanings to the underlined words.**

1. I need more money to <u>purchase</u> this computer.

a. buy b. create c. borrow d. discover

2. It was exciting to <u>observe</u> the growth of a frog.

a. own b. reach c. watch d. experience

Word Power

The prefix ob– is used to add the meaning of 'against,' 'toward,' or 'on.'
- I *object* to your use of bad language.
- We have overcome the first *obstacle*.

Pamukkale

Unit 10

• **Theme** > Places • **Reading Strategy** > Making inferences

◆ **What Do You Think?**

1. What is Turkey famous for?

2. Can you imagine a place that looks like a cotton castle?

◆ Background Knowledge ◆

The United Nations Educational, Scientific and Cultural Organization (UNESCO) was created in 1945. The agency chooses sites around the world that are important and unique. UNESCO has ten conditions to see if a site is culturally significant enough to become a "world heritage site." Currently, there are more than 900 UNESCO world heritage sites.

◆ Power Vocabulary ◆

• heritage	anything that has been handed down by tradition
• sacred	considered to be holy or connected with religion in a special way
• surroundings	the area around something
• thick	not thin; having parts closely crowded together
• mist	a thin fog near the ground
• historical	of or relating to the study of history
• distribute	to divide or spread
• interact	to act in close relation with one another
• remind	to cause to remember
• generation	all the people born and living during the same time

A Cotton Castle

T10

Magazine

Can you imagine what a castle made of cotton would look like? Well, there really is such a place in Turkey. It's called Pamukkale. Although its name means "cotton castle" in Turkish, it isn't really a castle and it isn't made of cotton. It's actually a beautiful natural area with a landscape of white rocks.

One of UNESCO's world heritage sites, Pamukkale is famous for sacred hot water springs and ancient buildings. These surroundings create a mysterious sense of beauty and peace. Water running down from higher areas creates a magical scene of clouds on the ground. Looking down, people seem to be swimming in pools of thick mist.

Pamukkale is also an important historical site. Mineral water from the springs is distributed into a body of water called the "Sacred Pool." This pool is located within the ruins of the ancient Greek city, Hierapolis. Swimming there is almost like interacting with the ancient Greeks.

People think there are also many health benefits from this water. It is said to improve a person's eyesight and skin, and to cure some illnesses. Pamukkale was chosen as a world heritage site because of these health benefits along with its natural, cultural, and historical significance.

Places like Pamukkale remind us of all the amazing things there are to see in the world. It must be protected and preserved so that future generations can enjoy the magic of the "cotton castle."

1st Reading _____ min _____ sec 2nd Reading _____ min _____ sec (237 words)

Making inferences ··· The writer's purpose or ideas are sometimes not stated directly in the passage. You can infer them from the context.

► What is the purpose of this article?

Reading Comprehension

Choose the best answers.

1. What is the passage mainly about?

a. the history of Pamukkale
b. the features of Pamukkale
c. famous world heritage sites
d. the formation of hot water springs

2. Which is NOT true according to the passage?

a. Pamukkale is famous for modern buildings.
b. Pamukkale is considered a world heritage site.
c. People can enjoy health benefits in the "Sacred Pool."
d. The Sacred Pool is located within the ruins of Hierapolis.

3. What does "Pamukkale" mean in Turkish?

a. cotton castle
b. cotton candy
c. hot water spring
d. wonderful place

4. Which is NOT thought to be a health benefit from the water of Pamukkale?

a. improving skin
b. improving muscles
c. curing illnesses
d. improving eyesight

5. What is mentioned as a reason to preserve Pamukkale?

a. to study the landscape
b. to save creatures in danger
c. to give local people money from the tourists
d. to allow future generations to enjoy the landscape

Write the answers in full sentences.

1. What is Pamukkale famous for?

____

2. Where is the mineral water from the hot water springs distributed into?

____

3. Why was Pamukkale chosen as a world heritage site?

____

Graphic Organizer

◆ **Fill in the blanks to explain Pamukkale.**

Pamukkale		
Surroundings	**Historical Value**	**Health Benefits**
• It is famous for __________ hot water springs and ancient buildings. • It creates a(n) __________ sense of beauty and peace.	• Spring water is distributed into the "Sacred Pool" within the __________ of the ancient Greek city, Hierapolis.	• Its spring water improves a person's __________ and __________, and helps to cure some __________.

Vocabulary Build-up

◆ **Choose the best words to fill in the blanks.**

1. I'm trying to get used to the __________ of my new neighborhood.

a. benefits b. heritages c. descriptions d. surroundings

2. Could you help me __________ the handouts to the students?

a. enjoy b. choose c. interact d. distribute

3. This picture __________ us of wonderful memories from our school days.

a. cures b. reminds c. protects d. preserves

◆ **Choose the words with similar meanings to the underlined words.**

1. In Hinduism, cows are <u>sacred</u> animals.

a. special b. blessed c. common d. ordinary

2. The room was filled with <u>thick</u> cigarette smoke.

a. thin b. slim c. heavy d. light

Word Power

The prefix dis– is used to add the meaning of 'away,' 'negative,' 'opposite of,' or 'separate.'

- I *dislike* horror movies.
- You can use this *discount* coupon at all outlets.

Soccer Matches

Unit 11

• Theme > Sports • Reading Strategy > Comparing and contrasting

What Do You Think?

1. Do you have any special memories of the World Cup?
2. How accurately can you predict the results of sports matches?

Background Knowledge

Pele, a former soccer player for Brazil, became well-known for his soccer predictions about twenty years ago. He is one of the best soccer players of all time, but his predictions are terrible. There is even a list online of his ten worst predictions, and people talk about "Pele's curse": the team or player who Pele says is particularly good often ends up performing terribly.

Power Vocabulary

• incredible	beyond belief or understanding
• predict	to say in advance that something will happen
• retire	to stop working, usually when getting to a certain age
• regard	to look upon or think of with a particular feeling
• former	what someone or something was in the past
• puzzle	to confuse
• cautious	being careful to escape from danger or trouble
• probable	likely to become true or real
• mention	to speak or notice something
• particular	unique or specific to a person or thing

Who Will Be the Winner?

T11

Newspaper

July 12, 2010 Oberhausen, Germany

After an incredible few weeks of correctly predicting eight soccer matches in the 2010 World Cup, Paul, the psychic octopus is retiring. His job was hardly stressful; he just had to choose between two food boxes with a flag on them. For example, for the Spain-Germany match, one box had the Spanish flag on it and the other had the German flag. The box Paul opened was regarded as his prediction for that game. He was very popular in Germany until he chose Spain to play in the finals instead of Germany. Then his former fans started talking about turning him into octopus soup.

However, Paul isn't perfect. During the 2008 European Championships he made four correct guesses out of five. Still, it's puzzling that Paul is better at this than a soccer player.

Pele, one of the best soccer players in history, is one of the worst soccer match predictors. Even Pele's former coach said that Pele knows nothing about soccer. Pele is more cautious now. During the 2010 World Cup he didn't pick any probable winners; he only said which teams he thought were the strongest. He mentioned Spain in particular, though, and they ended up winning the World Cup.

So who knows, maybe Pele has been taking lessons from Paul. In any case we wish Paul a happy retirement, safe from any octopus soup chefs.

(Paul died on October 26, 2010.)

1st Reading _____ min _____ sec   2nd Reading _____ min _____ sec (228 words)

Comparing and contrasting ··· Comparing and contrasting is used to show how certain things or ideas are similar or different from one another.

► What do Paul and Pele have in common?

Reading Comprehension

Choose the best answers.

1. What is the passage mainly about?

a. soccer predictions
b. the history of the World Cup
c. famous soccer players
d. the relationship between Pele and Paul

2. Who was Paul?

a. a psychic octopus
b. a sports announcer
c. a famous soccer player
d. a World Cup athlete

3. What was Paul's job?

a. putting on a show
b. coaching soccer players
c. cooking octopus soup
d. choosing between two food boxes

4. Which is NOT true according to the passage?

a. Pele is one of the best soccer players in history.
b. Pele is one of the best soccer predictors in history.
c. Paul picked Spain for the Spain-Germany match in 2010.
d. All of Paul's eight predictions came true for the 2010 World Cup.

5. What can be inferred from, "Then his former fans started talking about turning him into octopus soup," in lines 16-18?

a. Pele has taken a lesson from Paul.
b. More people came to like octopus soup.
c. Paul remained popular with soccer fans.
d. People were angry with Paul's prediction.

Write the answers in full sentences.

1. How many correct guesses did Paul make during the 2008 European Championships?

____

2. Which team did Pele mention as the strongest one in the 2010 World Cup?

____

3. Why did Pele's former coach say he knows nothing about soccer?

____

Graphic Organizer

◆ **Fill in the blanks to compare Paul and Pele as soccer match predictors.**

Soccer Match Predictors

Paul	Pele
• was a psychic ___________ • made predictions by choosing a food box with a(n) ___________ on it • made ___________ correct guesses out of five during the 2008 European Championships	• was one of the best ___________ players • was one of the worst soccer match ___________ • didn't pick any ___________ winners during the 2010 World Cup

Vocabulary Build-up

◆ **Choose the best words to fill in the blanks.**

1. At this point, no one can ___________ the results.

a. match b. mention c. perform d. predict

2. I saw the ___________ president in person yesterday.

a. former b. predictable c. incredible d. particular

3. My parents ___________ me as a child, even though I'm 19 years old.

a. retire b. regard c. puzzle d. mention

◆ **Choose the words with similar meanings to the underlined words.**

1. I try to be <u>cautious</u> when driving at night.

a. hasty b. reckless c. careful d. thoughtless

2. It is <u>probable</u> that my team will win the prize.

a. extra b. likely c. exact d. doubtful

Word Power

The suffix **-able** is used to add the meaning of 'capable of,' 'likely to,' or 'having.'

• My teacher is a *respectable* person.

• Grace is a very smart and *reasonable* woman.

Fermented Food

Unit 12

• Theme > Food • Reading Strategy > Skimming

◆ What Do You Think?

1. Do you know how to make cheese?
2. What are some examples of fermented food?

◆ Background Knowledge ◆

Cheese, wine, kimchi, and yogurt all have something in common: fermentation. Fermentation occurs when food grows yeast, or healthy bacteria. There are many different ways to make fermented food and drinks. When making cheese or yogurt, good bacteria are added to milk.

◆ Power Vocabulary ◆

• sour	having a sharp or acid taste
• appetizing	stimulating the desire for food or drink
• mix	to combine different things together
• purpose	the goal that someone wants to achieve
• unique	being the only one of a particular type
• process	a series of actions that produce a change or development
• digest	to change food into substances that the body can use
• immune	protected against a specific disease
• dairy	of or relating to the production of milk and milk products
• product	a thing created by someone or some process

Bulgarian Yogurt

Have you ever had sour milk? It doesn't sound appetizing, but a very similar food is enjoyed around the world: Bulgarian yogurt. Bulgarians have produced this yogurt for thousands of years.

Bulgarian yogurt was probably discovered by accident when someone left milk out too long and it mixed with bacteria. Later, people started to do this on purpose. This meant that they didn't have to worry about keeping their milk cold, and the result was delicious.

This yogurt contains two special kinds of bacteria. One kind is used in all yogurts. The other one is unique to Bulgaria and is named after the country. The bacteria are added to buffalo milk, goat's milk, or cow's milk. After the mixture sits out for a few hours or days, it turns into yogurt. This process is called fermentation.

Today, people in other countries make Bulgarian yogurt because of its health benefits. Like all fermented foods, it contains healthy bacteria that help us digest nutrients. These bacteria can also help fight against diseases like cancer. Fermented foods are good for the immune system, too.

There are hundreds of kinds of fermented food and drinks, and most of them can be found at the grocery store. There are dairy products like cheese and yogurt, and food products like *kimchi* and pickles. Whatever you choose, you can be sure it will be good for you!

1st Reading _____ min _____ sec   2nd Reading _____ min _____ sec (233 words)

Skimming ··· Skimming is used to quickly identify the main ideas of a text. Reading the first sentences of paragraphs can be a good way to summarize the main ideas in a text.

▶ What is the main idea of this article?

Reading Comprehension

Choose the best answers.

1. What is the passage mainly about?

a. where we get milk from
b. what Bulgarians eat for dessert
c. what happens during fermentation
d. the health benefits and process of making yogurt

2. What does this refer to in the passage?

a. tasting sour milk
b. choosing fresh food products
c. fighting against diseases like cancer
d. leaving milk out too long and it mixed with bacteria

3. Which is NOT a fermented food?

a. milk b. yogurt c. kimchi d. pickles

4. Why do people in other countries make Bulgarian yogurt?

a. because it is tasty
b. because it is easy to make
c. because it keeps people young
d. because it has many health benefits

5. Which is NOT mentioned as a benefit of fermented food?

a. helping digestion b. preventing the flu
c. fighting against cancer d. improving the immune system

Write the answers in full sentences.

1. How long have Bulgarians been making yogurt?

____

2. How was Bulgarian yogurt probably discovered?

____

3. What is found in all fermented foods?

____

Graphic Organizer

◆ **Fill in the blanks to explain Bulgarian yogurt.**

Bulgarian Yogurt

How Yogurt Is Made	Benefits of Yogurt
• goes through the process called ____________: add ____________ to milk → leave the ____________ for a few hours or days → turn into ____________	• ____________ healthy bacteria that help ____________ nutrients • helps fight against diseases like ____________ • is good for the ____________ system

Vocabulary Build-up

◆ **Choose the best words to fill in the blanks.**

1. Ryan thinks the result is more important than the ____________.

a. disease b. process c. appetite d. mixture

2. I often have a problem ____________ food when I'm nervous.

a. digesting b. producing c. fermenting d. discovering

3. When our ____________ system is weak, we can catch colds easily.

a. thick b. special c. immune d. nutrient

◆ **Choose the words with similar meanings to the underlined words.**

1. There were many <u>appetizing</u> dishes spread across the table.

a. pure b. common c. tasteless d. delicious

2. Anna showed her <u>unique</u> shoe designs at the fashion show.

a. broad b. general c. unusual d. similar

Word Power

The prefix pro– means 'for' or 'forward.'

- I'd like to *propose* a new method.
- There was rapid *progress* on the task.

Volunteer Doctors

Unit 13

• **Theme** > Social issues • **Reading Strategy** > Recognizing cause and effect

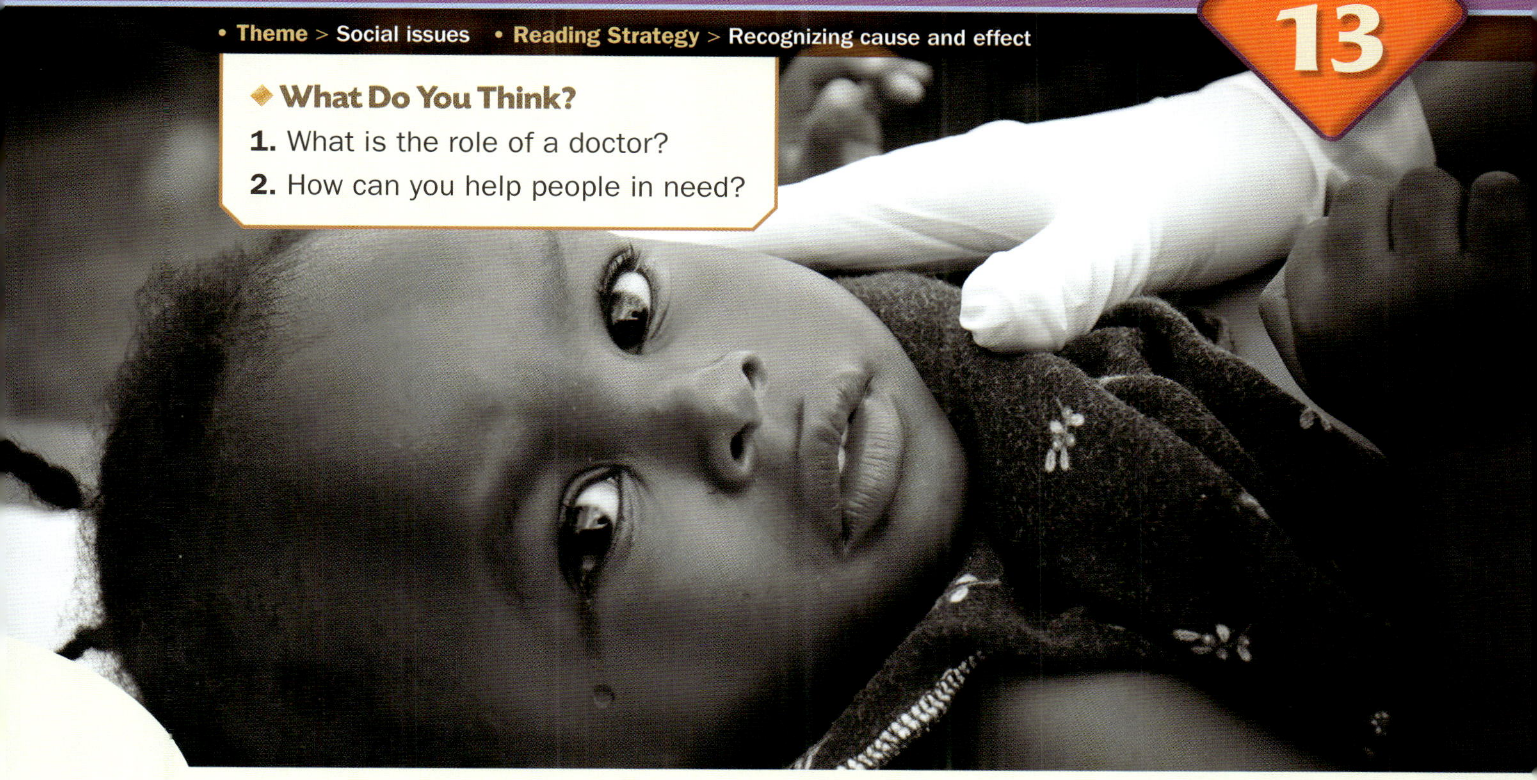

What Do You Think?

1. What is the role of a doctor?
2. How can you help people in need?

Background Knowledge

There are many people who cannot get even basic medical care. So in 1971, a group of French doctors started a program called Doctors Without Borders. It helps people in poor areas get medical care. Today, Doctors Without Borders is a worldwide organization. It trains volunteer doctors in more than 60 countries. In 1999, Doctors Without Borders won the Nobel Peace Prize for its humanitarian work.

Power Vocabulary

disaster	an event that causes great loss and misfortune
access	to reach, enter or use
volunteer	a person who performs a service willingly and without pay
attention	carefully listening to, looking at, or thinking about something
violence	physical force usually intended to cause injuries
supply	an amount of something available for use
aid	the work of providing treatment for someone or something
awareness	having knowledge of
organization	a group of people who work together
solve	to find the answer to a problem or question

Volunteer Doctors Heal the World

T13

In some parts of the world, people live in very poor conditions. They must deal with problems like natural disasters, war, and diseases. Medical treatments are not easy for these people to access. This is where volunteer doctors are needed. They visit these areas to give people medical attention.

Volunteer doctors visit struggling areas in places like South America and Africa. For example, there is a lot of violence and war in the Congo in Africa. People don't have medical care or basic supplies because of the ongoing fighting. Volunteer doctors provide medical care for patients who cannot pay for hospital visits. Volunteer doctors not only treat patients but also teach local doctors. Then, the local doctors can continue to give people medical aid when the volunteer doctors leave the area. Additionally, they educate people to increase their awareness of health issues. This helps prevent problems in the future. The United Nations Volunteers (UNV) and the Doctors Without Borders programs were designed to provide all three of these services.

International organizations like UNV and Doctors Without Borders help people who are in need all around the world. With their help, countries are becoming more aware of health issues, helping them slowly solve their problems. Volunteer doctors are sending a good message while helping the world with their healing hands.

1st Reading _____ min _____ sec 2nd Reading _____ min _____ sec (220 words)

Recognizing cause and effect ··· The cause and effect are the reason for and the result of an event. The cause makes the effect happen.

▶ Why do South America and Africa need volunteer doctors?

Reading Comprehension

Choose the best answers.

1. What is the passage mainly about?

a. natural disasters
b. the importance of health
c. traveling to South America
d. the roles of volunteer doctors

2. People in the Congo don't have medical care because of the ______________.

a. government　　b. ongoing fighting
c. bad weather　　d. volunteer doctors

3. Why do volunteer doctors visit struggling areas?

a. because patients don't trust local doctors
b. because volunteer doctors make more money
c. because patients cannot pay for hospital visits
d. because patients prefer volunteer doctors to paid doctors

4. Besides treating patients, what else do volunteer doctors do?

a. They raise babies.　　b. They collect money.
c. They build hospitals.　　d. They teach local doctors.

5. What can be concluded from the passage?

a. The number of doctors is increasing.
b. There needs to be more doctors all over the world.
c. Doctors should volunteer their services without any pay.
d. Volunteer doctors play an important role in the health of the world.

Write the answers in full sentences.

1. Where are volunteer doctors needed?

____

2. What are two international organizations of volunteer doctors?

____

3. What are the three services provided by volunteer doctors?

____

Graphic Organizer

◆ **Fill in the blanks to explain the roles of volunteer doctors.**

Roles of Volunteer Doctors

Targets	Services
• people who need medical care or ____________ supplies because of natural disasters or war	• provide ____________ care • teach ____________ doctors • educate people to increase awareness of ____________ issues

Vocabulary Build-up

◆ **Choose the best words to fill in the blanks.**

1. Their water ______________ ran short during the war.

a. supply b. disease c. messages d. hospitals

2. Many people are suffering because of unexpected natural ______________.

a. treatments b. attitude c. disasters d. attention

3. The group tries to raise ______________ about the dangers of smoking.

a. violence b. volunteers c. awareness d. organizations

◆ **Choose the words with similar meanings to the underlined words.**

1. I have to <u>solve</u> the problem myself by next Monday.

a. hand b. pass c. cause d. answer

2. The government gave people medical <u>aid</u> after the severe flood.

a. help b. aim c. goal d. decision

Word Power

The suffix -ness is used to add the meaning of 'quality of' or 'state of' to adjectives.

- My daughter's face lets us know how *happy* she is.
- My daughter's face was filled with joy and *happiness*.

Caves

Unit 14

• Theme > Geology • Reading Strategy > Drawing conclusions

◆ **What Do You Think?**

1. What is it like inside a cave?

2. How can people use caves?

◆ Background Knowledge ◆

Caves are natural underground places that are formed as a result of many years of environmental changes in the Earth. A few factors that have helped form caves are weather and time. Limestone, rock, and even glaciers made the caves that are found throughout the world today.

◆ Power Vocabulary ◆

• uncover	to make visible
• clue	evidence that helps to solve a problem
• practical	involving or relating to real situations and events
• shelter	a place where people are protected from bad weather or from danger
• escape	to get free from something; to get away
• store	to keep or put aside for future use
• lack	the state of not having something that a person needs or wants
• stable	not likely to fall apart or change
• temperature	the degree of heat or cold in a body or environment
• ancestor	a person who lived a long time ago

A Hidden World

T14

Scientists study caves to uncover a hidden world of human history. Research shows us that caves were used for a variety of reasons. Scientists have found cave paintings, pottery, tools, clothing, food, and human skeletons inside caves all over the world. These records provide historical information about humans from the past. They give us clues about the people who used and lived in caves.

Humans took advantage of caves for practical purposes. Since caves are closed off, humans used them for shelter and protection. They found caves to be safe areas. Some humans called these places home while thieves made them into places where they could escape from the law and hide stolen goods.

Humans also learned that caves were good places to store food. The dark and cool environment kept food fresh for a long time. You can consider them natural refrigerators! Thus, caves were used to store fruit, vegetables, aged cheese, and alcoholic drinks.

Caves had another important purpose, as well. The lack of sunlight and stable temperature were thought to be healthy. Therefore, caves were sometimes used as hospitals. Doctors believed that sick people would breathe better in them.

Researchers and scientists have discovered a lot about caves and their importance to humans. Besides these practical purposes, there is still more to learn. Now, caves are an important part of our studies to help us better understand our ancestors.

1st Reading _____ min _____ sec 2nd Reading _____ min _____ sec (232 words)

Drawing conclusions ··· After you read an article, you can draw conclusions from it by considering all the clues and facts given in the text.

▶ What conclusion did you draw from this passage?

Reading Comprehension

◆ Choose the best answers.

1. What is the passage mainly about?

a. the formation of caves
b. the definition of caves
c. the different types of caves
d. the practical purposes of caves

2. Why do scientists study caves today?

a. to study human history
b. to find treasures from the past
c. to uncover places to hide goods
d. to find new shelter and protection

3. Which does NOT fit in the blank?

Humans in the past used caves for ______________.

a. schools
b. shelters
c. hospitals
d. refrigerators

4. Why did humans use caves for protection?

a. because they are closed off
b. because they lack sunlight
c. because they are dark and cool
d. because they have a stable temperature

5. Caves were good for sick people because doctors thought ______________ in them.

a. people were safe
b. people would breathe better
c. people could hide things
d. people could store food fresh

◆ Write the answers in full sentences.

1. What have scientists found inside caves?

___

2. How did thieves use caves?

___

3. Why are caves important now?

___

Graphic Organizer

◆ **Fill in the blanks to explain how caves were used.**

Practical Purposes of Caves

Shelters	Storage	Hospitals
• Some humans used them for ________ because they are ________ areas. • Thieves used caves to ________ from the law.	• ________ and ________ environment kept food ________.	• Lack of ________ and ________ temperature were thought to be healthy.

Vocabulary Build-up

◆ **Choose the best words to fill in the blanks.**

1. You can expect ____________ economic growth this year.

a. stable b. practical c. historical d. academic

2. This tradition has been handed down to us from our ____________.

a. records b. ancestors c. protection d. information

3. People were provided with a safe ____________ during the natural disaster.

a. lack b. clue c. shelter d. importance

◆ **Choose the words with similar meanings to the underlined words.**

1. We have to <u>uncover</u> the truth to solve the case.

a. cover b. hide c. store d. reveal

2. You have to explain your <u>purpose</u> for the research.

a. law b. reason c. practice d. environment

Word Power

The prefix un– is used to add the meaning of 'not' to adjectives or verbs.

- David's words are *believable*.
- The news is *unbelievable*.

Mummies

Unit 15

• Theme > Mystery • Reading Strategy > Guessing word meaning

◆ **What Do You Think?**

1. What do you know about mummies?

2. What happens after people die?

◆ Background Knowledge ◆

Mummification is a process of preserving dead bodies. It was very popular in Egypt thousands of years ago. First, the Egyptians purified a person's dead body and removed his or her organs. Then, the body was dried out so no bacteria could enter and damage it. Finally, it was wrapped in bandages and decorated with jewelry.

◆ Power Vocabulary ◆

• tomb	a place where a dead person is buried
• ruin	to destroy completely
• belong	be owned by
• approximately	not precise but fairly close to being correct
• period	an amount of time
• separate	to divide into parts
• unite	to become one or joined
• spiritual	concerned with sacred matters, religion, or the church
• method	a way of doing something
• discovery	the act of finding something

Ancient Egyptian's Afterlife

Most of the ancient Egyptian tombs uncovered by archaeologists had been robbed or ruined by treasure hunters. One of the few tombs found nearly untouched belonged to Tutankhamen, or King Tut, an Egyptian pharaoh. However, pharaohs weren't the only people who were mummified. In fact, approximately 70 million people were mummified in Egypt over a period of almost 3,000 years. Mummification was popular because the Egyptians thought it helped the dead enter the afterlife safely.

The Egyptians thought that each person was made up of three different parts, which included the physical body, personality, and life-force. When a person died, the life-force and personality were separated from the physical body. However, the Egyptians also believed that all three parts had to be brought back together so that the dead could successfully move into the afterlife. They thought that mummification united all three parts. Bodies that were not reunited with their personality and life-force "died again" and had no hope of a new life.

Nowadays, mummification has lost its spiritual meaning, and it is no longer a common method of treating dead bodies. But the discovery of mummies from the past is still important. Finding and studying well-preserved mummies give us the opportunity to better understand what life was like in ancient Egypt.

1st Reading ____ min ____ sec 2nd Reading ____ min ____ sec (212 words)

Guessing word meaning ··· It takes time to look up every word you don't know. Sometimes the meaning of the word is explained in the previous or following sentence.

▶ What does the word 'reunited' mean in line **15**?

Reading Comprehension

Choose the best answers.

1. What is the passage mainly about?

a. an Egyptian pharaoh
b. ancient Egyptian tombs
c. treasure hunters from the past
d. mummification of ancient Egyptians

2. Which was NOT thought by Egyptians to be a part of a person?

a. body
b. afterlife
c. life-force
d. personality

3. What did ancient Egyptians think were separated from the body after death?

a. spirit and mind
b. spirit and life-force
c. personality and mind
d. life-force and personality

4. What was the purpose of mummification in ancient Egypt?

a. to show off wealth
b. to store treasures safely
c. to leave tombs untouched
d. to move successfully into the afterlife

5. Which is NOT true according to the passage?

a. Pharaohs were the only people who were mummified.
b. Mummies help people better understand ancient Egypt.
c. Most of the ancient Egyptian tombs had been robbed or ruined.
d. Mummification is not a common method of treating dead bodies anymore.

Write the answers in full sentences.

1. What happened to most ancient Egyptian tombs before they were discovered?

____

2. How did ancient Egyptians think the dead could move into the afterlife successfully?

____

3. Why is discovering mummies from the past important today?

____

Graphic Organizer

◆ **Fill in the blanks to explain Egyptians' beliefs about mummification.**

Beliefs about Mummification

- Each person is made up of ___________, ___________, and ___________.
- All three parts have to be brought back together to successfully move into the ___________.
- Mummification ___________ all three parts.

Vocabulary Build-up

◆ **Choose the best words to fill in the blanks.**

1. One foot is ______________ thirty centimeters.

a. safely b. likely c. probably d. approximately

2. Many ______________ were made by accident.

a. remains b. thieves c. shelters d. discoveries

3. You can get a 10% discount if you purchase it during this ______________.

a. hunter b. method c. period d. history

◆ **Choose the words with similar meanings to the underlined words.**

1. I <u>ruined</u> the surprise party because I couldn't keep it a secret.

a. kept b. forgot c. spoiled d. believed

2. The new department was made by <u>uniting</u> the three former departments.

a. joining b. dividing c. moving d. connecting

Word Power

The suffix -y is used to form nouns from verbs.
- I tried to *discover* more clues about the accident.
- Einstein made an important scientific *discovery*.

Animation

Unit 16

• Theme > Entertainment • Reading Strategy > Scanning

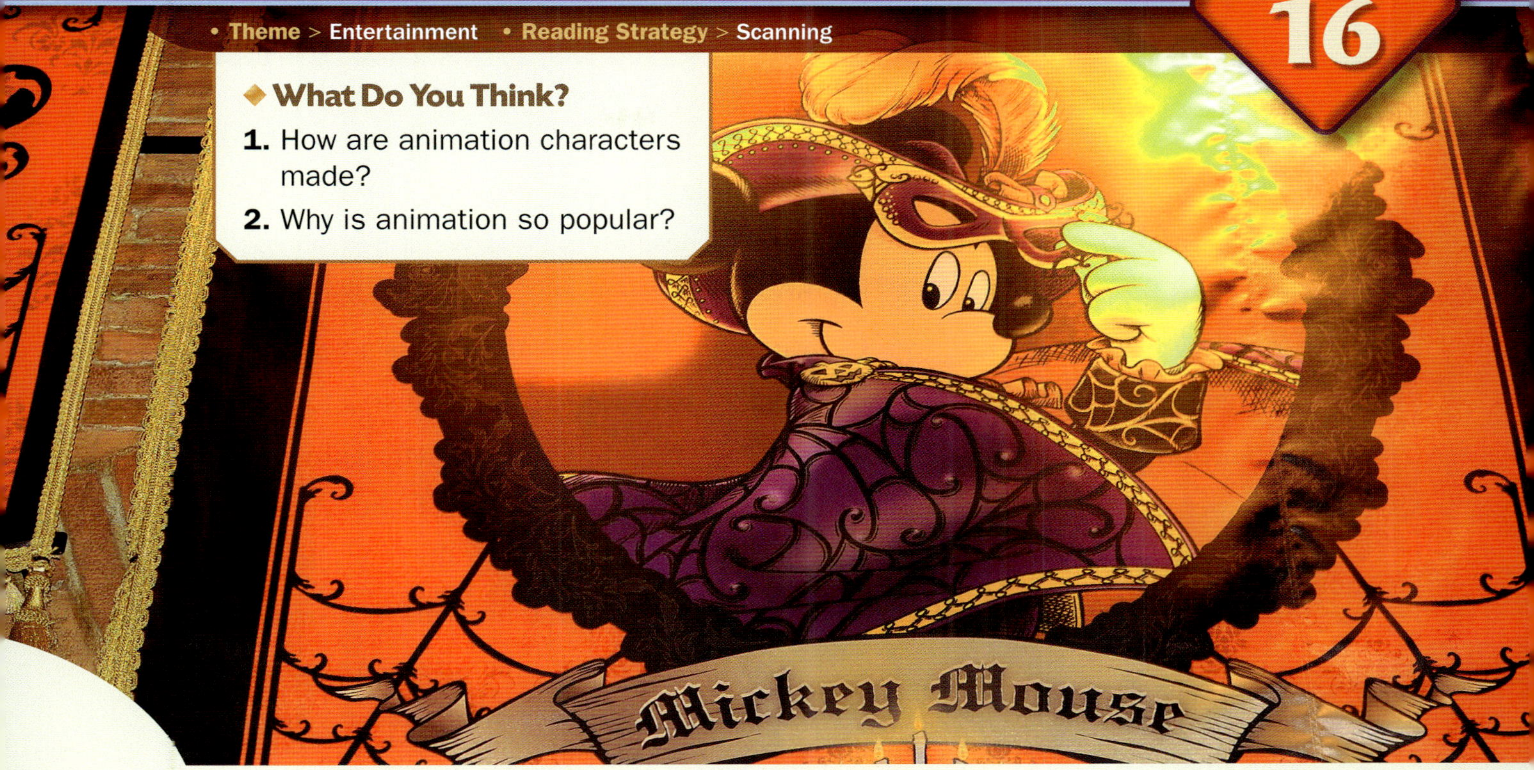

◆ **What Do You Think?**

1. How are animation characters made?
2. Why is animation so popular?

◆ Background Knowledge ◆

Animation is the process of making drawings or images appear to move within a film. Unlike most films, animation is made with drawings or computer graphics instead of actors. Artists start with one picture. Then they create many other similar pictures, changing the items in the picture little by little each time. When the images are shown in order very quickly, it looks like they are really moving.

◆ Power Vocabulary ◆

• traditional	based on old-fashioned ideas
• require	to have need of
• slightly	not very much, only a little
• motion	a change of position
• rely	to trust someone or something
• whole	all of something; not divided or broken
• enable	to give someone the ability to do something
• realistic	representing what is real
• silly	foolish; lacking seriousness
• appeal	to be attractive to

Taking Animation to a Whole New Level

T16

Do you have a favorite cartoon character? All around the world, most people know characters like Mickey Mouse, Donald Duck, and Shrek. But do you know how they were made? These characters were created by artists and then brought to life with the process of animation.

Traditional animation uses drawings or photo images. It is a very long and difficult process. It requires thousands of drawings to make just a few minutes of animation. Artists draw a series of pictures on clear plastic film, and they change each frame slightly to create motion. When all of these frames are shown one after the other, the characters seem to come alive. Mickey Mouse and Donald Duck were designed using the traditional animation process.

Thanks to the invention of computers, these characters are now drawn using computer animation. *Toy Story*, the first full-length computer animation, was made in 1995. Since then, filmmakers have begun to rely on computers. Computers have allowed them to take animation to a whole new level. Computers enabled artists to make thousands of images faster than before. They can create more realistic characters, items, and backgrounds than they could with hand drawings.

Animation has come a long way since its beginning. Once, it was thought to simply be silly entertainment for young children. But the realistic new movies being made with computer animation now appeal to people of all ages.

1st Reading ____ min ____ sec 2nd Reading ____ min ____ sec (233 words)

Scanning ··· Scanning is to look quickly at something without reading it carefully, often looking for some particular information such as key words or ideas. When you scan, do not read every word.

▶ What was the first full-length computer animation?

Reading Comprehension

Choose the best answers.

1. What is the passage mainly about?

a. the invention of computers
b. the development of animation
c. the success of the film *Toy Story*
d. the creation of the first animated characters

2. Where did artists draw pictures in the traditional animation process?

a. on canvas
b. on computers
c. in notepads
d. on clear plastic film

3. ____________ of drawings are required to make a few minutes of animation.

a. Tens
b. Millions
c. Thousands
d. Hundreds

4. Which is NOT true according to the passage?

a. Traditional animation is a fast and easy process.
b. Computers are now used to make animated movies.
c. Computer animation creates more realistic images.
d. Mickey Mouse was created using traditional animation.

5. Why does the passage mention *Toy Story*?

a. because it used traditional animated characters in a modern movie
b. because it earned more money than any other animated film in history
c. because it showed that traditional animation could be used to make movies
d. because it was the first full-length film to be made with computer animation

Write the answers in full sentences.

1. How do artists make traditional animation?

____

2. How were Mickey Mouse, Donald Duck, and Shrek brought to life?

____

3. What are the differences between traditional and computer animation?

____

Graphic Organizer

◆ **Fill in the blanks to compare traditional animation and computer animation.**

Animation

	Traditional Animation	Computer Animation
Making Process	• drawing a series of pictures on ______________ • changing frame slightly to create ______________ • characters coming alive	• making images on ______________ • creating more ______________ characters, items, and backgrounds
Audience	• young children	• ______________

Vocabulary Build-up

◆ **Choose the best words to fill in the blanks.**

1. My sister sleeps with her mouth ______________ open.

a. high　　b. slightly　　c. traditionally　　d. realistically

2. We replayed the same scene again in slow ______________.

a. series　　b. frame　　c. length　　d. motion

3. Set ______________ goals if you want to achieve them.

a. long　　b. wrong　　c. realistic　　d. enormous

◆ **Choose the words with similar meanings to the underlined words.**

1. Cole is hurt severely and requires immediate medical care.

a. allows　　b. needs　　c. pushes　　d. creates

2. Alisha always relies on luck instead of making an effort.

a. puts　　b. takes　　c. depends　　d. prepares

Word Power

The suffix -ic is used to form adjectives from nouns.

- The *base* of the industry is solid.
- I have a *basic* understanding of the problem.

Check Your Reading Speed

Draw a bar on the table below indicating the speed of your 1st and 2nd reading of the main passages.

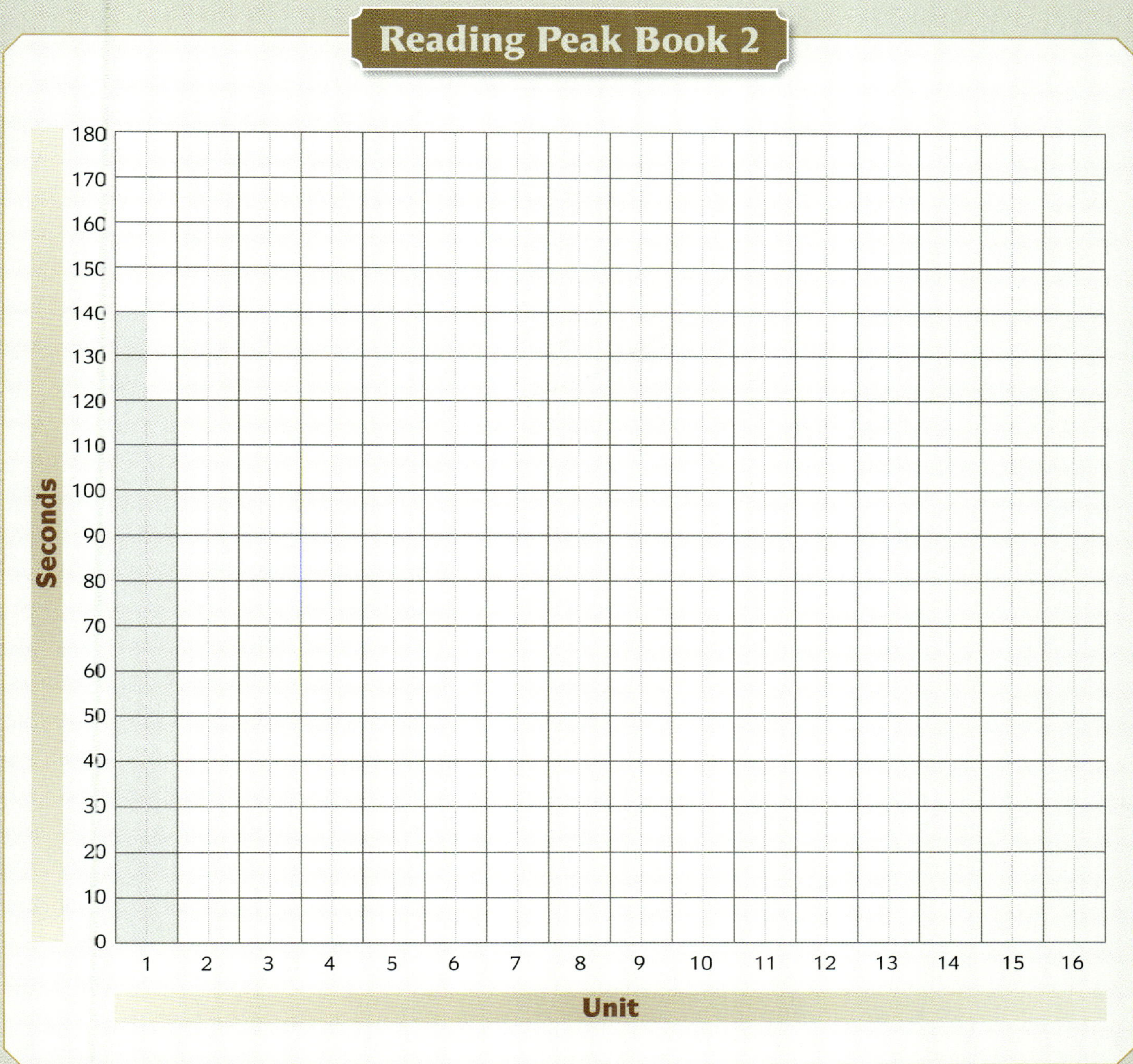

LEVEL GUIDE NE_Build & Grow Products

Category	Books	Lexile®	Kindergarten	Primary: Low Beginner	Primary: Beginner	Primary: High Beginner	Primary: Low Intermediate	Primary: Intermediate	Primary: High Intermediate	Secondary: A	Secondary: B	Components
Phonics	Phonics Show 1,2,3,4											Student Book/ Workbook/ 2 MultiROMs
Phonics	Phonics Show Readers 1,2,3,4											Book/ Audio CD
Phonics	Come On, Phonics 1, 2, 3, 4, 5											Student Book/ Workbook/ Readers/ DVD-ROM
Readers	Show Time											Student Book/ Workbook/ MultiROM
Coursebook	Come On, Everyone 1,2											Student Book/ Workbook/ Teacher's Book / DVD-ROM
Coursebook	Come On, Everyone 3,4											Student Book/ Workbook/ Teacher's Book / DVD-ROM
Coursebook	Come On, Everyone 5,6											Student Book/ Workbook/ Teacher's Book / DVD-ROM
Reading	Reading Sketch Starter 1,2,3	BR										Student Book/ Workbook/ MultiROM
Reading	Reading Sketch 1,2,3	170L~210L										Student Book/ Workbook/ Audio CD
Reading	Reading Sketch Up 1,2,3	260L~300L										Student Book/ Workbook/ Audio CD
Reading	Reading Sponge 1,2,3	160L~280L										Student Book/ Workbook/ MultiROM
Reading	Read & Retell 1,2,3	240L~390L										Student Book/ Workbook/ Audio CD
Reading	Reading Sense 1,2,3	320L~410L										Student Book/ Workbook/ Audio CD
Reading	Reading Clue 1,2,3	490L~510L										Student Book/ Workbook/ Audio CD
Reading	The Basic Way 1,2,3 (2nd Edition)	570L~660L										Student Book/ Workbook/ MultiROM
Reading	Read to Reach 1,2,3	600L~660L										Student Book/ Workbook/ Audio CD
Reading	The Best Way 1,2,3 (2nd Edition)	860L~970L										Student Book/ Workbook/ MultiROM
Reading	Reading Source 1,2,3	580L~710L										Student Book/ Workbook/ Audio CD

Reading Peak 2

WORKBOOK

NE_Build & Grow

WORKBOOK

Reading Peak 2

NE_Build & Grow

Unit 01

Lie Detectors

Vocabulary Practice

A. Write the best word for each sentence. Change its form if necessary.

sweat   heartbeat   response   permit   suspect

1. The policeman chased the ______________ down the street.
2. Did you check if this cafe ______________ smoking?
3. My ______________ was racing when I saw Stella in person.
4. I felt energized after I ran and ______________ a lot.
5. People had a positive ______________ to our campaign.

B. Choose the best word for each blank.

1. I can't ______________ red from green, so I can't drive a car.
   a. see   b. tell   c. ask   d. show
2. You can ______________ the height of this table using a ruler.
   a. detect   b. research   c. measure   d. breathe
3. Mike wants to work in the marketing ______________ of this company.
   a. response   b. apartment   c. evidence   d. department
4. The scientist is trying to ______________ a medicine to cure the disease.
   a. invent   b. expect   c. destroy   d. abandon
5. Jack was thought to be ______________ of the crime.
   a. able   b. wide   c. basic   d. guilty

C. Write the best phrase for each sentence. Change its form if necessary.

whether ... or not   be able to   tell a lie

1. My face turns red when I ______________.
2. I ______________ speak Spanish and English.
3. ______________ Lynda will come ______________ is important to me.

Writing Practice

A. Change the sentences as in the example.

Ex Lie detectors are widely rejected, but they are still used in some places.
→ **Even though** lie detectors are widely rejected, they are still used in some places.

1. I told the truth, but Issac wouldn't believe me.
→ ______________________________

2. I heard the news, but I hid it from my friends.
→ ______________________________

3. I practiced the violin very hard, but I couldn't do well at the concert.
→ ______________________________

B. Match the sentence parts.

1. The polygraph can detect whether •	• a. if you had a machine.
2. No person or machine is able •	• b. to detect lies 100 percent of the time.
3. There is also a problem •	• c. by John Larson and Leonarde Keeler.
4. How useful it would be •	• d. the person is lying or not.
5. The polygraph was invented •	• e. with using lie detectors.

C. Make the sentences with the given words and write them.

1. (tell / is / someone / can / A machine / if / lying).
→ ______________________________

2. (why / most countries / permit / lie detector / is / results / This / don't).
→ ______________________________

3. (a lie, / telling / When / body response / people / will / their / are / change).
→ ______________________________

4. (The interviewer / questions / a crime / asks / about).
→ ______________________________

5. (when / nervous / take / Innocent people / they / to / have / a lie detector test / get).
→ ______________________________

Unit 02

Ancient Greece

Vocabulary Practice

A. Write the best word for each sentence. Change its form if necessary.

state courage government advantage fit

1. The major ______________ is its strength.
2. We need support from the ______________ to get rid of school violence.
3. The company changed the product to ______________ the new requirements.
4. In a(n) ______________ of war, many children lose their parents.
5. Jake stood in front of a bear in order to show off his ______________.

B. Choose the best word for each blank.

1. The warriors showed their ______________ by writing in blood.
   a. history b. problems c. loyalty d. training
2. You have to take care of both your mental and ______________ health.
   a. physical b. effective c. brutal d. dependent
3. Young children need ______________ attention and affection.
   a. little b. official c. constant d. occasional
4. If you ______________ one thing, you lose something.
   a. train b. gain c. envy d. leave
5. No one wants to do the ______________ work but someone has to.
   a. weak b. little c. steady d. tough

C. Write the best phrase for each sentence. Change its form if necessary.

the moment get used to go through

1. You will soon ______________ your new friends.
2. The airplane took off ______________ I arrived at the terminal.
3. All the new workers need to ______________ an intensive training course.

Writing Practice

A. Change the sentences as in the example.

Ex It was as hard for boys as girls at these schools.
→ It was **harder** for boys **than** girls at these schools.

1. Hawaii is as beautiful as the Mediterranean.
→ ______________________________

2. The movie is as interesting as this book.
→ ______________________________

3. The Christmas tree is as tall as my sister.
→ ______________________________

B. Match the sentence parts.

1. This let the boys get •	• a. to both boys and girls.
2. Boys joined the "Agoge," •	• b. used to hunger.
3. The Spartan education was taught •	• c. which taught them war songs.
4. Sparta produced the best warriors •	• d. to become a Spartan warrior.
5. The babies were physically fit enough •	• e. among the 20 polises in ancient Greece.

C. Make the sentences with the given words and write them.

1. (would / Spartans / strong women / believed / strong babies / that / bear).
→ ______________________________

2. (land / There / to / constant / were / gain / battles).
→ ______________________________

3. (was / left / If / a baby / they / die / thought / was / to / too weak, / it).
→ ______________________________

4. (women / to / and / Girls / their / protect / had / homes).
→ ______________________________

5. (an advantage / was / during / times / Their tough education / war / of).
→ ______________________________

Unit 03

Beavers

Vocabulary Practice

A. Write the best word for each sentence. Change its form if necessary.

attract gap construct flood leave

1. The cast of the movie ______________ many viewers.
2. Please ______________ some cookies for your brother.
3. Some people couldn't escape the sudden ______________ this summer.
4. The mouse entered through a(n) ______________ between the wall and floor.
5. Nancy dreams of ______________ her own house in the countryside.

B. Choose the best word for each blank.

1. Overfishing can destroy the ______________ of the sea.
   a. depth b. economy c. disaster d. ecosystem
2. All creatures have ways to ______________ and escape danger.
   a. hurt b. survive c. serve d. provide
3. It was the most horrible natural ______________ in Canada.
   a. disaster b. pattern c. branch d. entrance
4. My mother exercises every morning to ______________ her health.
   a. build b. break c. produce d. maintain
5. This town provides a good ______________ for seniors to live in.
   a. paw b. role c. result d. environment

C. Write the best phrase for each sentence. Change its form if necessary.

such as stop … from play a role in

1. Austin's words ______________ my decision.
2. Mia likes outdoor activities, ______________ hiking and camping.
3. I didn't want to ______________ him ______________ leaving.

Writing Practice

A. Change the sentences as in the example.

Ex Swimming underwater is difficult for other animals.

➡ **It** is difficult **for** other animals **to swim** underwater.

1. Understanding my parents fully is difficult for me.

➡ ______________________________

2. Reading John's feelings is not hard for me.

➡ ______________________________

3. Waking up early in the morning is easy for Emma.

➡ ______________________________

B. Match the sentence parts.

1. Beavers maintain water systems •	• a. them from enemies.
2. These dams attract other animals •	• b. to hurt the environment.
3. Beavers need dams to protect •	• c. for beavers to live in.
4. The homes are safe places •	• d. that live in or near water.
5. The trees cut down by beavers seem •	• e. by constructing dams and lodges.

C. Make the sentences with the given words and write them.

1. (fill / Beavers / to / mud / in / the gaps / use).

➡ ______________________________

2. (underneath / have / the water / These homes / entrances).

➡ ______________________________

3. (enough, / build / lodges / high / beavers / is / When / the water level).

➡ ______________________________

4. (dams and lodges / beavers / for / safe homes / provides / of / The construction).

➡ ______________________________

5. (stop / from / Dams / floods / homes / destroying / their).

➡ ______________________________

Unit 04

Ultraviolet Light

Vocabulary Practice

A. Write the best word for each sentence. Change its form if necessary.

cause capable shield cell surface

1. I'm ______________ of taking care of myself.
2. The ______________ of the road is not smooth.
3. Every new organism begins as a single ______________.
4. A cigarette carelessly thrown away can ______________ a forest fire.
5. The children used a tree to ______________ them from the rain.

B. Choose the best word for each blank.

1. Smoking is very ______________ to your health.
   a. mild b. vital c. bright d. harmful
2. Tom was pleased to see the bright ______________ of sunlight.
   a. rays b. ways c. colors d. length
3. The huge log ______________ the entrance to the building.
   a. burned b. blocked c. included d. protected
4. I had nothing to ______________ myself from the strong wind.
   a. mean b. reach c. travel d. protect
5. If you don't avoid strong sunlight, it'll ______________ your skin.
   a. glow b. wear c. damage d. pollute

C. Write the best phrase for each sentence. Change its form if necessary.

be responsible for pass through be capable of

1. We have to ______________ three tunnels to get there.
2. Who ______________ this new project?
3. You ______________ solving the problem on your own.

Writing Practice

A. Change the sentences as in the example.

Ex The ozone layer is like a gas shield around the Earth. It blocks UV rays.

➡ The ozone layer is like a gas shield around the Earth **that** blocks UV rays.

1. I'm reading a book. It was written by a famous novelist.

   ➡ ______________________________

2. Sean joined the club. It is one of the most popular in his school.

   ➡ ______________________________

3. I wore my new hat. It was given to me by my friend Julie.

   ➡ ______________________________

B. Match the sentence parts.

1. It's still important •	• a. from sunburns.
2. How is UV light different •	• b. in the aging of the skin.
3. Sunscreen doesn't just protect you •	• c. to wear sunscreen.
4. UV light has shorter wavelengths •	• d. from normal light?
5. UVA rays play a major role •	• e. than visible light.

C. Make the sentences with the given words and write them.

1. (the surface / UVB rays / reach / the skin / of).

   ➡ ______________________________

2. (doesn't / from / UVA and UVB / This / rays / safe / mean / we're).

   ➡ ______________________________

3. (protect / of / your skin cells / from / skin cancer / It / the greater danger / can).

   ➡ ______________________________

4. (into / UVA rays / of / are / passing / the skin / capable).

   ➡ ______________________________

5. (changes / because / harmful / it / is / can / in / the cells / It / cause).

   ➡ ______________________________

Unit 05

Greek Mythology

Vocabulary Practice

A. Write the best word for each sentence. Change its form if necessary.

influence present notice athlete stem

1. Did you ______________ the smile on Sara's face?
2. A lot of folk songs ______________ from a local legend or myth.
3. How many people were ______________ at the party?
4. I don't think her opinion has a(n) ______________ on my actions.
5. Rebecca was a great ______________ who won a gold medal in the Olympics.

B. Choose the best word for each blank.

1. I failed to ______________ to the Internet five times.
   a. pick b. raise c. catch d. connect
2. That actor has a mysterious ______________ about him.
   a. crown b. charm c. fairy d. chance
3. I ______________ with Anne but she would not listen to me.
   a. cried b. pleased c. pleaded d. released
4. It seemed like a(n) ______________ before Brian appeared.
   a. hour b. moment c. eternity d. incident
5. One man ______________ after the thief but couldn't catch him.
   a. took b. looked c. pulled d. chased

C. Write the best phrase for each sentence. Change its form if necessary.

fall in love be known for in honor of

1. I went to a dinner ______________ Angela's retirement.
2. It is romantic to ______________ with a stranger.
3. Australia ______________ its beautiful natural sites.

Writing Practice

A. Change the sentences as in the example.

Ex You have noticed that the winners of marathons wear laurel crowns.
→ **Have you noticed** that the winners of marathons wear laurel crowns?

1. You have tasted meat pie.
→ ______________________________

2. You have built a building with bricks.
→ ______________________________

3. You have been to Paris and visited the Louvre.
→ ______________________________

B. Match the sentence parts.

1. Greek mythology is •
2. Apollo pleaded for a woman •
3. Aphrodite became angry •
4. Laurel crowns are connected •
5. Daphne's father turned her •

• a. to love him back.
• b. because Apollo did not love her back.
• c. present in our everyday lives.
• d. to Greek mythology.
• e. into a laurel tree so she could be safe.

C. Make the sentences with the given words and write them.

1. (Eros / love / anyone / fall / make / in / could).
→ ______________________________

2. (from / He / after / but / she / Daphne / ran away / him / chased).
→ ______________________________

3. (to / make / Aphrodite / Eros / fall / love / Apollo / in / commanded).
→ ______________________________

4. (stem / crowns / of / from / Apollo and Daphne / the story / These).
→ ______________________________

5. (to / and / great athletes / Apollo / laurel crowns / poets / gave).
→ ______________________________

Unit 06

UFOs

Vocabulary Practice

A. Write the best word for each sentence. Change its form if necessary.

debate announce astronomer report exist

1. We expect to ______________ the results next week.
2. Let's end the ______________ and put this to a vote.
3. You have to check the weather ______________ before going out.
4. The comet was named after the British ______________ Edmund Halley.
5. Various opportunities ______________ for students to get a scholarship.

B. Choose the best word for each blank.

1. We have a(n) ______________ friendship that no one could break.
   a. solid b. weak c. minor d. impossible
2. I ______________ your message but forgot to reply.
   a. visited b. received c. proved d. believed
3. I've been ______________ busy since my vacation.
   a. eternally b. eventually c. extremely d. roughly
4. If you ______________ to eat fatty food, you'll be overweight.
   a. stop b. develop c. consider d. continue
5. This science fiction movie is about a war between people and ______________.
   a. tutors b. aliens c. friends d. reporters

C. Write the best phrase for each sentence. Change its form if necessary.

mistake … for not long ago find out

1. I want to ______________ exactly what happened at the party.
2. I met Daisy ______________ but she can't remember me.
3. I ______________ the sugar ______________ the salt and added it to my soup.

Writing Practice

A. Change the sentences as in the example.

Ex Had aliens really come to the Earth?
→ They tried to find out **if aliens had really come** to the Earth.

1. Are there any health problems?
→ You have to check ______________________

2. Can you come to the party on time?
→ I want to know ______________________

3. Has Christine been to any foreign countries?
→ I wonder ______________________

B. Match the sentence parts.

1. It wasn't long ago	•	• a. that aliens have never visited.
2. People could mistake a cloud	•	• b. for an alien spaceship.
3. Most reports of UFOs are from people	•	• c. that people were more serious.
4. Astronomers are experts	•	• d. on the night sky.
5. It's impossible to prove	•	• e. who don't know about astronomy.

C. Make the sentences with the given words and write them.

1. (are / Astronomers, / who / firm / study / these kinds of / things, / very).
→ ______________________

2. (UFOs / Scientists / evidence / don't / that / exist / lack).
→ ______________________

3. (that / They / UFOs / there / announced / evidence / was / no / of).
→ ______________________

4. (has / astronomer / ever / seeing / reported / a UFO / No).
→ ______________________

5. (received / The U.S. military / in / reports / many / UFOs / the 1940s / of).
→ ______________________

Unit 07

Five Senses

Vocabulary Practice

A. Write the best word for each sentence. Change its form if necessary.

vary | recognize | depend | survive | shake

1. No one can ______________ my firm determination.
2. Some passengers ______________ the plane crash.
3. Laws ______________ from state to state in the U.S.
4. I hadn't see her for a long time, but I could ______________ her at first sight.
5. Whether we'll go on a picnic or not ______________ on the weather.

B. Choose the best word for each blank.

1. Smartphones provide a new way for people to ______________.
   a. create   b. sense   c. exercise   d. communicate
2. The shepherd is passing by with a(n) ______________ of cattle.
   a. herd   b. pile   c. number   d. amount
3. The company is proud of the ______________ quality of its products.
   a. weak   b. poor   c. enormous   d. superior
4. This contest would be a good chance to show your ______________.
   a. nature   b. ability   c. creature   d. supplies
5. I can ______________ people's voices without seeing their faces.
   a. vary   b. spend   c. distinguish   d. experience

C. Write the best phrase for each sentence. Change its form if necessary.

give birth | according to | have a hard time

1. You can choose your lunch ______________ your taste.
2. My dog Sammy ______________ to five puppies yesterday.
3. Try going for a short walk when you ______________ concentrating.

Writing Practice

A. Change the sentences as in the example.

Ex Humans wouldn't have a hard time trying to live in the world with senses.
→ **Without** senses, humans **would have** a hard time trying to live in the world.

1. You can buy a ticket with money.
→ ______________________________

2. I can stay warm with a jacket.
→ ______________________________

3. Mary can get good grades at school with a great tutor.
→ ______________________________

B. Match the sentence parts.

1. Their sounds help them • • a. to distinguish herd members.
2. The mother can recognize • • b. depending on environment.
3. Elephants' nostrils are used • • c. as an example.
4. Certain senses develop in a unique way • • d. escape from dangerous situations.
5. We can take elephants' senses • • e. her baby from this smell.

C. Make the sentences with the given words and write them.

1. (different / is / The value / every creature / of / for / each sense).
→ ______________________________

2. (where / can / rainwater / tell / They / is).
→ ______________________________

3. (drops / her dung / A mother elephant / a pile of / into / her baby elephant).
→ ______________________________

4. (Senses / things / to / are / necessary / used / gather).
→ ______________________________

5. (is / out of / on land / thought / to be / Their hearing / the best / all the creatures).
→ ______________________________

Unit 08

Operas Vs. Musicals

Vocabulary Practice

A. Write the best word for each sentence. Change its form if necessary.

dialog   inspire   element   costume   audience

1. Health is an essential ______________ of happiness.
2. Traveling to the sea ______________ me to write a great poem.
3. I gave Jessica a fancy stage ______________ in honor of her debut.
4. The movie became popular because of its touching ______________.
5. The singer was disappointed that there were only ten people in the ______________.

B. Choose the best word for each blank.

1. I always ______________ magic for my children's birthday parties.
   a. compose   b. perform   c. attend   d. stand
2. Four rising stars were cast as the main ______________ of the movie.
   a. singers   b. features   c. characters   d. background
3. Jason opened a ______________ big restaurant, but it had only a few customers.
   a. poorly   b. fairly   c. hopefully   d. probably
4. Environmental changes can have a ______________ effect on the ecosystem.
   a. realistic   b. creative   c. dramatic   d. comical
5. His diligence and patience are vital ______________ of Sean's success.
   a. goals   b. results   c. processes   d. elements

C. Write the best phrase for each sentence. Change its form if necessary.

in front of   even though   both ... and

1. I become nervous when I'm ______________ a large audience.
2. ______________ you're not interested, you should attend the seminar.
3. I think ______________ you ______________ I are responsible for the problem.

Writing Practice

A. Change the sentences as in the example.

Ex The music halls often have microphones. And musicals are performed there.
→ The music halls **where** musicals are performed often have microphones.

1. I visited the town. And I was born there 12 years ago.
→ ______________________________

2. I had dinner at a restaurant. And the view there was great.
→ ______________________________

3. Let's look for a shop. And you can buy clothes there.
→ ______________________________

B. Match the sentence parts.

1. Early musicals were inspired •
2. Most operas performed were •
3. Performers playing the characters •
4. Musicals have a lighter vocal style •
5. Have you ever heard •

• a. than operas.
• b. of *The Phantom of the Opera*?
• c. by light operas.
• d. sing the dialog very loudly.
• e. written before the 1920s.

C. Make the sentences with the given words and write them.

1. (older / are / than / musicals / much / Operas).
→ ______________________________

2. (they / where / have / The music halls / performed / microphones / are).
→ ______________________________

3. (in 1879 / musicals / performed / were / The first / on Broadway).
→ ______________________________

4. (elements / Most musicals / have / comical / although / they / are / sad).
→ ______________________________

5. (performed / a stage / are / Both / and / operas / on / musicals).
→ ______________________________

Unit 09

Ecotourism

Vocabulary Practice

A. Write the best word for each sentence. Change its form if necessary.

reach　experience　community　pure　adventure

1. I want to ______________ a free lifestyle.
2. I will stick to my decision until I ______________ my goal.
3. Traveling in Africa was a thrilling ______________ for Jackie.
4. I can breathe ______________ air at the top of the mountain.
5. There are many free classes offered at the ______________ center.

B. Choose the best word for each blank.

1. I like people with a ______________ heart.
   a. pure　b. local　c. alien　d. necessary
2. Tim dreams of ______________ his own house someday.
   a. owning　b. fixing　c. selling　d. destroying
3. I ______________ some clothes and forgot to get the receipt.
   a. spent　b. produced　c. brought　d. purchased
4. You can see different kinds of ______________ such as cars and bicycles.
   a. races　b. vehicles　c. machines　d. riverbanks
5. The swamp was ______________ for environmental research.
   a. decided　b. provided　c. preserved　d. discovered

C. Write the best phrase for each sentence. Change its form if necessary.

look back on　go on a trip　contribute to

1. My parents greatly ______________ my success.
2. Let's ______________ to the sea if the weather is nice.
3. If you ______________ your past, you will figure out what to do next.

Writing Practice

A. Change the sentences as in the example.

Ex I helped save the landscape. It was created 350 million years ago.
→ I helped save the landscape **which** was created 350 million years ago.

1. Chen is fighting against the disease. It makes him weak.
→ ______________________________

2. I bought a pot at the flea market. It was held this week.
→ ______________________________

3. I'm listening to music. It was written by my cousin.
→ ______________________________

B. Match the sentence parts.

1. Ecotourism brings people to •	• a. owned by local people.
2. We were delighted •	• b. to contribute to the economy.
3. He took us around the small shops •	• c. my children experience heaven.
4. We also traveled •	• d. places that have not been changed.
5. I hope ecotourism will help •	• e. into the area's untouched forests.

C. Make the sentences with the given words and write them.

1. (an ecotourism trip / on / I / decided / go / to / Charlevoix / to).
→ ______________________________

2. (nature / to / It / its / pure state / observe / in / exciting / was).
→ ______________________________

3. (was / One / experience / of / to / my dreams / untouched nature).
→ ______________________________

4. (our tour guide / us / When / reached / we / welcomed / our destination).
→ ______________________________

5. (smile / Charlevoix / Looking / on / back / me / our trip / to / makes).
→ ______________________________

Unit 10

Pamukkale

Vocabulary Practice

A. Write the best word for each sentence. Change its form if necessary.

ancient   improve   cure   surroundings   heritage

1. The ______________ of my house are very peaceful.
2. UNESCO selects many places as cultural or natural ______________ sites.
3. Jordan wants to be a doctor who ______________ diseases.
4. I'm highly interested in the history of ______________ Egypt.
5. I have some ideas of how we could ______________ our school.

B. Choose the best word for each blank.

1. I saw heavy ______________ around the mountaintop.
   a. mist   b. trees   c. land   d. leaves
2. My family has lived here for three ______________.
   a. consumers   b. athletes   c. parents   d. generations
3. We traveled to China and visited some ______________ places.
   a. present   b. medical   c. historical   d. economical
4. The Internet enables people to ______________ with others all over the world.
   a. respond   b. attract   c. interact   d. predict
5. Kevin arrived at the ______________ of the accident after hearing the news.
   a. site   b. cause   c. spring   d. image

C. Write the best phrase for each sentence. Change its form if necessary.

be famous for   remind ... of   be made of

1. These items ______________ metal and are very hard.
2. I just called to ______________ you ______________ of our appointment.
3. The president ______________ his fluent speech and generous smile.

Writing Practice

A. Change the sentences as in the example.

Ex Pamukkale must be protected. Then future generations can enjoy it.
→ Pamukkale must be protected **so that** future generations **can** enjoy it.

1. People need to pay attention to this problem. Then society can be a better place.
→ ______________________________

2. The writer must actually visit the city. Then the story can be more realistic.
→ ______________________________

3. Bicycles got lighter and more compact. Then people could carry them at all times.
→ ______________________________

B. Match the sentence parts.

1. Swimming there is almost like •	• a. for sacred hot water springs.
2. Pamukkale was chosen •	• b. of all the amazing things.
3. Pamukkale is famous •	• c. interacting with the ancient Greeks.
4. Places like Pamukkale remind us •	• d. with a landscape of white rocks.
5. It's a beautiful natural area •	• e. as a world heritage site.

C. Make the sentences with the given words and write them.

1. (People / be / swimming / seem / thick mist / in / to / pools / of).
→ ______________________________

2. (within / pool / of / is / the ruins / This / the ancient Greek city / located).
→ ______________________________

3. (The water / to / a person's eyesight / said / improve / is).
→ ______________________________

4. (These / surroundings / of / beauty and peace / create / a mysterious sense).
→ ______________________________

5. (is / from / distributed / Mineral water / a body of water / the springs / into).
→ ______________________________

Unit 11 Soccer Match

Vocabulary Practice

A. Write the best word for each sentence. Change its form if necessary.

incredible former probable cautious mention

1. It's quite ______________ that it'll snow tonight.
2. The news is so ______________ that I can't believe it.
3. Of the two choices, the ______________ seems more sensible.
4. Be ______________, or you might hurt yourself.
5. Don't ______________ what your children did wrong too often.

B. Choose the best word for each blank.

1. I came home from work to watch a tennis ______________.
   a. major b. match c. chef d. flag
2. At the moment, we can't ______________ who will win this game.
   a. predict b. represent c. protect d. remind
3. Many people are concerned about what they will do after they ______________.
   a. fire b. hire c. retire d. guess
4. If I had to ______________ my favorite hobby, I'd say it's reading.
   a. pick b. pack c. locate d. expect
5. I can't fully understand several ______________ passages in this article.
   a. safe b. probable c. exciting d. puzzling

C. Write the best phrase for each sentence. Change its form if necessary.

instead of end up in particular

1. I like all kinds of sports, but I like soccer ______________.
2. I hope they will ______________ living happily together.
3. Jake chose Sue ______________ me as a dance partner.

Writing Practice

A. Change the sentences as in the example.

Ex The fact that Paul is better at this than a soccer player is puzzling.
→ **It's puzzling that** Paul is better at this than a soccer player.

1. The fact that my team will win the finals is certain.
→ ______________________________

2. The fact that my purse is missing is strange.
→ ______________________________

3. The fact that the criminal went to prison is natural.
→ ______________________________

B. Match the sentence parts.

1. Paul just had to choose •	• a. the worst soccer match predictors.
2. His former fans started •	• b. between two food boxes.
3. The box was regarded •	• c. winning the World Cup.
4. Pele is one of •	• d. as his prediction for that game.
5. Spain ended up •	• e. talking about octopus soup.

C. Make the sentences with the given words and write them.

1. (chose / Paul / very popular / he / was / until / Spain).
→ ______________________________

2. (out / Paul / four / five / of / correct guesses / made).
→ ______________________________

3. (been / Maybe / has / lessons / from / Paul / taking / Pele).
→ ______________________________

4. (Pele / Pele's former coach / nothing / that / knows / about / said / soccer).
→ ______________________________

5. (the strongest / Pele / which / he / thought / said / teams / were).
→ ______________________________

Unit 12 Fermented Food

Vocabulary Practice

A. Write the best word for each sentence. Change its form if necessary.

add digest appetizing nutrient product

1. We have to try to meet the demand for the new ________________.
2. The smell of baking bread from the bakery was quite ________________.
3. If you lie down right after eating, it's not easy to ________________.
4. Getting enough ________________ is important for a baby to be healthy.
5. I mixed two eggs and some flour, and then ________________ some salt.

B. Choose the best word for each blank.

1. Bronze is a ________________ of copper and tin.
   a. grocery b. mixture c. disease d. maximum
2. Her name is so ________________ that it is easy to remember.
   a. long b. difficult c. unique d. delicious
3. When you choose food, you have to carefully check what it ________________.
   a. digests b. fights c. discovers d. contains
4. I'm allergic to ________________ foods such as milk, butter, and ice cream.
   a. dairy b. daily c. simple d. healthy
5. The ordering ________________ of this online shopping mall is too long.
   a. root b. flight c. process d. purpose

C. Write the best phrase for each sentence. Change its form if necessary.

by accident be named after on purpose

1. Harrison ________________ his father, Harry.
2. The Kellogg brothers discovered corn flakes ________________.
3. Jenny got angry because she thought I lost the key ________________.

Writing Practice

A. Change the sentences as in the example.

Ex What you choose doesn't matter. You can be sure it will be good for you.
→ **Whatever** you choose, you can be sure it will be good for you.

1. What I tell him doesn't matter. He won't believe me.
→ ______________________________
2. What you want doesn't matter. It will happen.
→ ______________________________
3. What you do doesn't matter. I won't leave you.
→ ______________________________

B. Match the sentence parts.

1. Bulgarian yogurt was • • a. to buffalo milk.
2. This meant that • • b. because of its health benefits.
3. The bacteria are added • • c. after the country.
4. People make Bulgarian yogurt • • d. they didn't have to worry.
5. The other one is named • • e. probably discovered by accident.

C. Make the sentences with the given words and write them.

1. (bacteria / special kinds / two / This yogurt / of / contains).
→ ______________________________
2. (doesn't / Sour milk / appetizing / sound).
→ ______________________________
3. (kinds of / There / fermented food / are / hundreds of).
→ ______________________________
4. (have / Bulgarians / for / thousands of / this yogurt / years / produced).
→ ______________________________
5. (fight / diseases / can / help / also / These bacteria / against).
→ ______________________________

Unit 13

Volunteer Doctors

Vocabulary Practice

A. Write the best word for each sentence. Change its form if necessary.

supply   volunteer   increase   attention   aid

1. We're trying to find a way to ______________ sales of this camera.
2. Carter ______________ at the hospital twice a week.
3. Our water ______________ is low because of the drought.
4. Once Jack focuses on something, he never turns his ______________ to other things.
5. When someone gets hurt, first ______________ is very important.

B. Choose the best word for each blank.

1. Everyone can ______________ this public toilet easily.
   a. heal   b. access   c. solve   d. prevent
2. You should go for regular ______________ checkups to stay healthy.
   a. basic   b. medical   c. local   d. additional
3. The patient didn't get any better after receiving the ______________.
   a. issue   b. design   c. country   d. treatment
4. Ted works for an international nonprofit ______________.
   a. condition   b. disaster   c. patient   d. organization
5. Action movies with too much ______________ can be harmful to children.
   a. service   b. healing   c. violence   d. messages

C. Write the best phrase for each sentence. Change its form if necessary.

in need   deal with   be aware of

1. Tina is able to ______________ upset customers very well.
2. You need to ______________ the problems our company is facing.
3. Tim looked around to see if any other people were ______________ of help.

Writing Practice

A. Change the sentences as in the example.

Ex Volunteer doctors treat patients. They also teach local doctors.
→ Volunteer doctors **not only** treat patients **but also** teach local doctors.

1. I like sunny days. I also like rainy days.
→ ______________________________

2. Allie works during the day. She also works at night.
→ ______________________________

3. The accident took hundreds of lives. It also destroyed lots of property.
→ ______________________________

B. Match the sentence parts.

1. Medical treatments are not easy	• •	a. of health issues.
2. They are sending a good message	• •	b. for these people to access.
3. Countries are becoming more aware	• •	c. problems like natural disasters.
4. The local doctors can continue	• •	d. while helping the world.
5. They must deal with	• •	e. to give people medical aid.

C. Make the sentences with the given words and write them.

1. (where / This / are / volunteer doctors / needed / is).
→ ______________________________

2. (visit / people / medical attention / give / these areas / Volunteer doctors / to).
→ ______________________________

3. (a lot of / and / war / in / the Congo / There / in / is / violence).
→ ______________________________

4. (The programs / to / designed / were / these services / provide).
→ ______________________________

5. (people / help / are / in / who / International organizations / need).
→ ______________________________

Unit 14

Caves

Vocabulary Practice

A. Write the best word for each sentence. Change its form if necessary.

practical escape temperature shelter breathe

1. Brad ______________ deeply before he dove into the sea.
2. Everybody needs food, ______________, and clothing.
3. Let's sit down together and make a(n) ______________ plan.
4. The criminal tried to ______________ to another country.
5. The average ______________ was around 4 degrees below zero last winter.

B. Choose the best word for each blank.

1. We are hoping for ______________ economic conditions.
   a. strict b. stable c. ongoing d. continuous
2. A ______________ of food can cause people to die of hunger.
   a. lack b. diseases c. variety d. richness
3. It is said the mammoth is the ______________ of the modern-day elephant.
   a. fossil b. god c. ancestor d. descendant
4. No ______________ has been found yet that could help solve the problem.
   a. clue b. puzzle c. question d. word
5. After harvesting it, the farmer ______________ the wheat in the barn.
   a. stole b. stored c. used d. planted

C. Write the best phrase for each sentence. Change its form if necessary.

a variety of as well take advantage of

1. I would like to visit ______________ countries after I retire.
2. You need to ______________ the opportunities you are given.
3. You can learn from success. You can learn from failure, ______________.

Writing Practice

A. Change the sentences as in the example.

Ex Caves are closed off, so humans used them for shelter and protection.
→ **Since** caves are closed off, humans used them for shelter and protection.

1. It was sunny, so we decided to go for a walk.
→ ______________________________

2. Our team won the prize, so we had a party.
→ ______________________________

3. Her favorite soda was on sale, so Emma bought two bottles of it.
→ ______________________________

B. Match the sentence parts.

1. Humans took advantage •	• a. from the law.
2. Thieves could escape •	• b. of caves for practical purposes.
3. The lack of sunlight •	• c. to be safe areas.
4. Humans found caves •	• d. was thought to be healthy.
5. You can consider caves •	• e. natural refrigerators.

C. Make the sentences with the given words and write them.

1. (used / shelter / Humans / for / and / caves / protection).
→ ______________________________

2. (clues / These records / the people / lived / us / about / who / in / caves / give).
→ ______________________________

3. (learned / to / good places / that / Humans / store / were / food / caves).
→ ______________________________

4. (food / a long time / The dark and cool / kept / environment / for / fresh).
→ ______________________________

5. (shows / Research / that / for / caves / were / used / reasons / us / a variety of).
→ ______________________________

Unit 15

Mummies

Vocabulary Practice

A. Write the best word for each sentence. Change its form if necessary.

opportunity lack method ruin separate

1. If you tell her, it will ______________ the surprise.
2. I'm grateful for the ______________ to take on this job.
3. The Tasman Sea ______________ Australia from New Zealand.
4. I'm very tired from a(n) ______________ of sleep over the last few days.
5. Teachers are looking for more efficient ______________ of teaching.

B. Choose the best word for each blank.

1. Now it is a(n) ______________ belief that the Earth is round.
   a. rare b. dead c. common d. ancient
2. The Dalai Lama is the ______________ leader of Tibet.
   a. spiritual b. physical c. untouched d. mechanical
3. England and Scotland were ______________ into one kingdom.
   a. pointed b. united c. passed d. created
4. The ______________ of America changed history.
   a. pharaoh b. afterlife c. discovery d. personality
5. The police heard about someone planning to ______________ a bank.
   a. rob b. lose c. reunite d. include

C. Write the best phrase for each sentence. Change its form if necessary.

be made up of belong to no longer

1. We ______________ the same health club downtown.
2. Since the fight, I ______________ have any contact with Amy.
3. The U.K. ______________ England, Wales, Scotland, and Northern Ireland.

Writing Practice

A. Change the sentences as in the example.

Ex He has three parts. They include the physical body, personality, and life-force.
→ He has three parts, **which** include the physical body, personality, and life-force.

1. I heard the result. It shocked me.
→ ______________________________

2. I got a gift from Sam. I lost it.
→ ______________________________

3. My parents always say cheerful words. They make me happy.
→ ______________________________

B. Match the sentence parts.

1. The ancient Egyptian tombs had •	• a. separated from the physical body.
2. The Egyptians thought it helped •	• b. been robbed or ruined.
3. The dead could successfully move •	• c. of three different parts.
4. Each person was made up •	• d. the dead enter the afterlife.
5. The life-force and personality were •	• e. into the afterlife.

C. Make the sentences with the given words and write them.

1. (the few tombs / Tutankhamen / untouched / One / to / of / belonged / found).
→ ______________________________

2. (be / All three parts / back / to / brought / together / had).
→ ______________________________

3. (us / the opportunity / Mummies / to / our ancestors / give / better understand).
→ ______________________________

4. (important / the past / mummies / The discovery / is / of / from).
→ ______________________________

5. (longer / treating / dead bodies / a common method / is / of / Mummification / no).
→ ______________________________

Unit 16

Animation

Vocabulary Practice

A. Write the best word for each sentence. Change its form if necessary.

appeal realistic invention slightly whole

1. The mouse was a wonderful ______________.
2. The book is certain to ______________ to most readers.
3. You can view the ______________ city from the top of the tower.
4. To make your dream come true, first set a(n) ______________ goal.
5. Your delivery has been ______________ delayed due to the traffic jam.

B. Choose the best word for each blank.

1. You can enjoy all the activities, or ______________ lie on the beach.
   a. simply b. hardly c. lately d. interestingly
2. Please stop calling me that ______________ nickname.
   a. silly b. creative c. realistic d. attractive
3. A kimono is a ______________ Japanese costume.
   a. modern b. realistic c. personal d. traditional
4. Money will ______________ you to do anything you want.
   a. enable b. engage c. require d. need
5. We hope it will ______________ lifelong relationships.
   a. ruin b. destroy c. create d. loosen

C. Write the best phrase for each sentence. Change its form if necessary.

thanks to rely on a series of

1. ______________ failures didn't discourage the athlete.
2. Many lives have been saved ______________ seatbelts.
3. I'm pleased to have made a good friend to ______________.

Writing Practice

A. Change the sentences as in the example.

Ex With computers, characters are drawn using computer animation.
→ **Thanks to** computers, characters are drawn using computer animation.

1. With her high grades, Samantha was able to get a great job.
→ ____________________

2. With the advanced technology, the price of sugar became cheaper.
→ ____________________

3. With the use of the new antibiotic, the spread of the virus has been stopped.
→ ____________________

B. Match the sentence parts.

1. These characters were	•	• a. to people of all ages.
2. Artists draw a series of pictures	•	• b. created by artists.
3. The realistic new movies appeal	•	• c. like Mickey Mouse and Shrek.
4. It requires thousands of drawings	•	• d. on clear plastic film.
5. Most people know characters	•	• e. to make just a few minutes of animation.

C. Make the sentences with the given words and write them.

1. (begun / Filmmakers / on / have / to / computers / rely).
→ ____________________

2. (Animation / since / has / come / a long way / its beginning).
→ ____________________

3. (the first / was / computer animation, / full-length / *Toy Story*, / made / in 1995).
→ ____________________

4. (each frame / They / create / slightly / change / to / motion).
→ ____________________

5. (animation / or / photo images / uses / Traditional / drawings).
→ ____________________

Word List

Unit 01

- expression
- invent
- measure
- response
- innocent
- guilty
- permit
- evidence
- reject
- department

Unit 02

- state
- constant
- gain
- bear
- courage
- loyalty
- brutal
- advantage
- enemy
- envy

Unit 03

- glance
- vital
- maintain
- construct
- pile
- gap
- steady
- flood
- entrance
- endanger

Unit 04

- ray
- visible
- cause
- cell
- responsible
- surface
- capable
- severely
- shield
- block

Unit 05

- present
- influence
- connect
- stem
- command
- plead
- chase
- eternity
- honor
- athlete

Unit 06

- alien
- astronomer
- exist

- announce
- mistake
- debate
- prove
- solid
- firm
- continue

Unit 07

- essential
- survive
- communication
- vary
- depend
- superior
- creature
- distinguish
- herd
- recognize

Unit 08

- perform
- costume
- audience
- composer
- tragic
- character
- dialog
- element
- inspire
- fairly

Unit 09

- reach
- local
- purchase
- contribute
- landscape
- fuel
- observe
- pure
- preserve
- community

Unit 10

- heritage
- sacred
- surroundings
- thick
- mist
- historical
- distribute
- interact
- remind
- generation

Unit 11

- incredible
- predict
- retire
- regard
- former
- puzzle
- cautious

- probable
- mention
- particular

Unit 12

- sour
- appetizing
- mix
- purpose
- unique
- process
- digest
- immune
- dairy
- product

Unit 13

- disaster
- access
- volunteer
- attention
- violence
- supply
- aid
- awareness
- organization
- solve

Unit 14

- uncover
- clue
- practical
- shelter
- escape
- store
- lack
- stable
- temperature
- ancestor

Unit 15

- tomb
- ruin
- belong
- approximately
- period
- separate
- unite
- spiritual
- method
- discovery

Unit 16

- traditional
- require
- slightly
- motion
- rely
- whole
- enable
- realistic
- silly
- appeal

Aqua

Reading Peak Aqua is a three-level nonfiction reading series designed for intermediate to high intermediate students. Compelling topics motivate students and make reading exercises informative and meaningful. This series presents background knowledge passages to ensure a better understanding of topics while engaging the interest of readers. All readings are based on carefully considered word lists to expand students' vocabulary and develop their reading fluency. This series includes reading comprehension questions to enhance students' critical thinking skills. With *Reading Peak Aqua*, students are ready to become advanced readers.

Features:

- Engaging, academic nonfiction readings in various forms of writing
- Interesting, informative background knowledge
- Exercises to improve reading speed
- Open-ended questions that strengthen students' thinking and writing skills
- Basic reading strategies accompanied by simple exercises
- Level-appropriate word lists and definitions before each main reading
- Graphic organizers to support students' mind mapping abilities
- Workbook for more vocabulary, grammar, and writing practice

Components:

Student Book / Workbook / Audio CD

Online Resources: www.nebooks.co.kr (Korean) / www.nebuildandgrow.com (English)

MP3 files / Vocabulary lists / Answer keys and translations

Reading Peak Aqua Series:

[190~210 words]

[220~240 words]

[250~270 words]

	Title	Lexile	Components
	Reading Peak 1,2,3	860L~900L	Audio CD
	Read Up 1,2,3	1070L~1320L	Student Book/ Supplementary Material/ MP3 CD
	Subject Link Starter 1,2,3	430L~460L	Student Book/ Workbook/ MultiROM
	Subject Link 1,2,3	520L~610L	Student Book/ Workbook/ Audio CD
	Subject Link 4,5,6	720L~830L	Student Book/ Workbook/ Audio CD
	Subject Link 7,8,9	860L~950L	Student Book/ Workbook/ Audio CD
Listening	Listening Seed 1,2,3		Student Book/ Workbook/ Scripts & Answer Keys/ Audio CD
	Listening Season 1,2,3 [1st Edition]		Student Book/ Workbook/ Scripts & Answer Keys/ MP3 CD
	Listening Season 1,2,3 [2nd Edition]		Student Book/ Workbook/ Scripts & Answer Keys/ MultiROM
	Listening Planner 1,2,3		Student Book/ Workbook/ Scripts & Answer Keys/ MP3 CD
Writing	Write Right Beginner 1,2,3		Student Book/ Workbook
	Write Right 1,2,3		Student Book/ Workbook
	Write Right Paragraph to Essay 1,2,3		Student Book/ Workbook
Speaking	Everyone, Speak! Kids 1,2,3		Student Book/ Workbook/ MultiROM
	Everyone, Speak! Beginner 1,2,3		Student Book/ Workbook/ MultiROM
	Everyone, Speak! 1,2,3		Student Book/ Workbook/ MultiROM
Grammar	Grammar Space Kids 1,2,3		Student Book/ Workbook
	Grammar Space Beginner 1,2,3		Student Book/ Workbook
	Grammar Space 1,2,3		Student Book/ Workbook
	Grammar in Mind 1,2,3		Student Book/ Workbook
	Grammar in Focus 1,2,3		Student Book/ Workbook/ Audio CD
	Grammar Effect 1,2,3		Student Book/ Workbook